TALES OF
TRIUMPH
MOTORCYCLES
& THE MERIDEN FACTORY

First published in 1996 by Veloce Publishing Plc, 33 Trinity Street, Dorchester, Dorset DT1 1TT, England. Fax: 01305 268864/E-mail: veloce@veloce.co.uk/Website: www.veloce.co.uk. Reprinted 1996. This paperback edition published in 2000. Reprinted 2000.
ISBN: 1 901295 67 2/UPC:36847-00167-4

Visit Veloce on the Web - www.veloce.co.uk

TALES OF
TRIUMPH
MOTORCYCLES
& THE MERIDEN FACTORY

HUGHIE HANCOX

VELOCE PUBLISHING PLC
PUBLISHERS OF FINE AUTOMOTIVE BOOKS

Acknowledgements

This story is an attempt to convey to the reader the wonderful atmosphere that prevailed at Meriden - where the greatest motorcycle in the world was made - in the 1950s, how things slowly changed throughout the 1960s and, finally, in the early Seventies, how it all came to a terrible and ignominious end ...

Many of the people I have written about are, sadly, no longer alive, but their names and faces are vivid in my memory and hardly a day passes without my thinking of them during the course of my restoration work.

Thanks to my wife, Gloria, who has suffered my motorcycle mania for many years, and thanks to both John Nelson and Jack Wickes for their invaluable help.

In memory of Leslie Derek "Nobby" Clarke and Alex Scobie, my good friends.

Hughie Hancox
Coventry, England

Contents

The Repair Shop

Mr Sidney Tubb, ex-pre-war TT rider and finishing shop foreman, inspecting a 1960 American T120 on the B range track.

My story starts one foggy November evening in 1953. I was sitting in the deserted factory canteen at Meriden, listening to the cooks prepare the meal for the next day. As I sat anxiously awaiting the arrival of the man who was going to interview me, Mr Sidney Tubb, finishing shop manager, I looked around and tried to imagine the now darkened canteen fully lit and bustling with workers, some queuing, some sat at the long tables eating and chatting. The whole atmosphere was so different from the small dingy shop where I was currently employed as a motorcycle mechanic, working all hours with no proper supervision for the princely sum of 26 shillings (£1.30) a week.

I had worked there for almost a year when my father called in one day and was shocked to see the working conditions. The 'workshop' was a cobbled floor building with no toilets or washing facilities of any kind. That meant no handwashing from eight o'clock in the morning until six at night, and then I cycled home the six-and-a-half miles in my overalls, dirty hands and all! There was a quick turnover of fitters — no one seemed to last more than a few weeks — so I had no proper supervision at all.

Then one day, a fire broke out! The pot-bellied stove erupted all over the oily floor, setting alight two bikes awaiting repairs, plus some overalls on a stool. Due to my keenness I suppose, I jumped straight in and tackled the blaze with some old sacks and the overalls I was wearing. I managed to push the two flaming bikes outside into the drive, burning my hands, eyebrows and (much to my mother's annoyance) my jumper. By this time, the alarm had been raised and the showroom salesman came to my aid with a bucket of sand and the only fire extinguisher we had.

We finally put out the fire and, when I returned from hospital after having my hands bandaged, I was summoned to the manager's office. Thinking I was in for a congratulatory pat on the back (and maybe even an extra five shillings in my pay packet that week), I was astonished to be given a telling-off for not letting the place burn down! Needless to say, when I arrived home that evening, burned, bandaged and, worse, with great holes in my jumper, my father was furious. So, on the following day, he visited the shop, gave the manager a piece of his mind and took me home, cancelling my indentures.

So, there I was, out of a job and all I knew was that I had to get back amongst bikes, by hook or by crook. Now, my father, having owned various motorcycles in his youth, had lived next door to Mr & Mrs Fred Wickes, who had a son and daughter. The son's name was Jack. He and my father were good friends and they often worked together on my father's bike or just sat and talked motorcycles. Jack's father was despatch manager at the Dale Street Works of Triumph Motorcycles, Coventry so, obviously, when Jack came of age, he went to work there, too.

Being a bright young spark, he was soon recognized as having great potential and before long was arriving home on works bikes. By this time my father was interested in replacing his 350cc machine with a 500 and, after a word with Jack and his father, an opportunity presented itself when a 1935 model 5/5 became available. It was one of the 1935 International Six Day Trials machines, returned to the factory for rectification and conversion back to standard road trim, before being offered for sale. (Many years later, I discovered that the bike had been ridden by Alan Jefferies, then a works trials and road racer for Triumph. It's funny how things have a way of turning up for, many years later in 1965, Alan Jefferies' son, Tony, became my apprentice at Meriden and, in 1978, I restored for the National Motorcycle Museum the 1935 model 5/10 racer ridden by Alan Jefferies in the Isle of Man TT!)

So, with the help of Mr Wickes and his son, Jack, my father was able to purchase this super-fast 500cc twin-port machine. Years later, when I owned my 1952 Tiger 100, he would say to me, "My model 5/5 would do ninety any time, anywhere — so where's the progress?"

A few years later, Jack and my father lost touch, I suppose because they found girlfriends and later on got married, with Jack moving to one side of Coventry and my father to the other, and it wasn't until the night I arrived home, burnt and bandaged, that Jack's name cropped up again in our household. Dad still had his address, so off we went to see him. It was quite a reunion and somewhere in the conversation, amongst the "Do you remember when we ...?" and "What was her name?" reminiscences, a job for me was mentioned. After saying goodnight, we set off home with a promise from Jack that he would see if he could sort something out for me. I had never felt so elated and the reflections in the bus windows and the bright lights of the street lamps seemed to echo my mood. It was only a few weeks to Christmas and everything was going to be great; I just knew it!

Sure enough, Jack sent word and I went to his house — on my own, this time — riding my newly-acquired 500cc Ariel Red Hunter. I was trembling with apprehension as I knocked on his door, hardly able to think straight. He opened the door, having heard my bike, and asked me into the living room. By now I was almost bursting. Then he said it: "You have to go to Meriden for an interview and, provided you satisfy them, you will be offered the position of trainee for a period of seven years". I couldn't believe it! Working at Meriden, it was like a dream come true. I knew I hadn't had the interview yet, but somehow that seemed a mere formality, because something told me deep down inside that I would get that job; I just knew I would.

So, here we are again, sitting in the darkened canteen, awaiting the arrival of Mr Sidney Tubb, full of collywobbles and feeling not quite as sure of myself

The young Jack Wickes pictured in 1959.

Tales of Triumph & Meriden

The 1955 'plunger' Cub. It was finished in Shell Blue Sheen with black raised centre ribs on the front and rear guards with white pinstriping. Wheel centres were Shell Blue Sheen with black pinstriping.

as before. I needn't have worried, however, as Mr Tubb was a pleasant man, small with grey hair and a balding pate, a fresh complexion and wearing a smart grey suit. Even after 36 years I can remember every detail of him. Little of the conversation, however, remains, as I answered his questions automatically without even thinking about them. There were, I remember, some compulsory maths questions — percentages and so on — but, apart from these, my memory is a blank until he said "Well, young man, you seem to be alright, so I'll take you along to meet the manager of the shop you will be working in."

With that he rose, smiled and bade me follow him. We went out of the canteen into the cold, damp, misty night air; by this time it was about 5.15pm. Somehow November nights, back in the Fifties, seemed darker and foggier than they do now! We walked across the factory yard, past the push-bike and motorcycle sheds and up the slope to the rubber swing doors at the top, leading into the finishing shop. As he pushed open one of the doors and walked through, I followed, but wasn't prepared for the sight, sound and smell of that place. It was breathtaking, to say the least. The workers were knocking off and, consequently, there was a lot of good-natured shouting and banter as they put away their things and struggled into riding suits, washed hands and did all the things that chaps do when they have finished a day's work and are preparing to go home. I suppose this callow youth got a few stares as we walked up the main gangway, between row-upon-row of gleaming machines. My mouth must have been wide open; I had never seen so many bikes, there were hundreds of them! Silver Tiger 100s, maroon Speed Twins, metallic blue Thunderbirds and the new Shell Blue Sheen swinging-arm Tigers! But it was the smell of new rubber, paint and petrol — as well as the sights and sounds —

which was simply marvellous to my mind. I just couldn't take it all in!

The finishing shop was huge and in it was housed the main track; rectification area; electrical area, where the wiring looms were fitted; the testers' area, where bikes were prepared for road test, and the CKD area, where the bikes were partially dismantled for crating and shipment abroad. Interspersed amongst all these were workbenches and lockers which, to my inexperienced eyes, looked as though they had been placed willy-nilly. Later on, I found these made up various sections, all with their own gang, chargehand and foreman.

We passed through the main shop, past the Cub and Terrier track, past the paint shop and experimental area until we finally turned a corner — and we were there. This was the service repair department. "The most important department in the factory," I was told, in no uncertain manner, by its manager Mr A St J Masters, whom I now faced across a desk. Standing until after the introduction had been completed and Mr Tubb had left, Mr Masters asked me to take a seat, just as Mr Fields the foreman entered.

Having been given a brief history of my background by Jack Wickes, they knew that I had already worked for a short while in a motorcycle agency, so it was with great firmness that Mr Masters spoke the words that have stuck in my mind to this day: "Young man, there are three ways to accomplish a job on a motorcycle: the right way, the wrong way and the Triumph way. It would

The rectification area. This photo was taken on a work's gala open day.

therefore be beneficial for you to forget the first two and do your utmost to remember the third!" I nodded an acknowledgement, though I hardly understood what he meant as it seemed to contradict all that my dad had said to me before. When doing a job at home I'd often ask him, "What's the best and easiest way of doing this?" to which he would often reply "The right way."

In the ensuing months, there was a certain amount of confusion in my mind over this line of thought, as would often be the case when I was carrying out work on my own, like overhauling a cylinder head. Joe Bosworth would be getting on with the rest of the engine, leaving me to replace guides, cut seats and grind in new valves. Finally, I would carry out a petrol test down the ports to determine whether the seats were 100 per cent. After completing the allocated job I would ask Joe to check it for me, saying "Is this good enough?" to which he would reply "Good enough isn't near enough. Do it again." After doing the job again and testing it with petrol I'd ask "Is this near enough?" and Joe would say "Yes — that's good enough!" Totally confusing to a young chap trying his hardest!

I drifted off into thought and remembered one of Dad's jokes that seemed appropriate. It was a little like the old village blacksmith tink-tinkling away with his hammer on a job, periodically gripping it with a pair of tongs and pushing it down into the white-hot coals of his furnace. When a bunch of American tourists came round to visit they stopped and, after taking pictures of him at work, watched him with interest. One big American said "Gee, fella we've got machines in the States that do this work to 10/1000th of an inch." The old smithy stopped hammering, looked at him, hawked and spat in the fire, before remarking "That be no good here — here you've got to be dead on!"

Mr Masters spoke again, jolting me from my reverie, "I hope you will like working here, there are opportunities for willing chaps." I recollect mumbling my thanks before being ushered out by Mr Fields and taken the next few paces into the workshop proper. And what a workshop, especially after the one I had just come from: you could eat a meal off the floor it was so clean. All the work trestles were at right angles to the one long steel-topped workbench down the left-hand wall, each section of bench being punctuated by a vice.

I remember that there were about 14 or 15 spaces running down towards the bottom of the repair shop, with the most senior fitters being at the top. The man who was to become my foreman in later years, Herbert Victor Carter, was on the top bench — number 1. Next to him was Ken Nichols, a small wiry Birmingham chap who rode a sprung hub Thunderbird and Garrard single-seater sidecar. After Ken, was good old Ted Russell, a Cornishman, solid as a rock, who fought at Tobruk, Mersah Metruh and El Alamein in Montgomery's Eighth Army. He was six feet in height and just about the same width! He rode his combo from Snitterfield on the outskirts of Stratford-on-Avon every day and back again for as long as I knew him. Next to him was Joe Bosworth, ex-boxer, ex-mountain grasstracker, ex-scrambler, ex-speedway rider and the man to whom I was to be seconded for the next six months.

Following down the line after Joe was Harold Dix, affectionately known as Dixie, and after him Benny Marshall, real name Zenon Marzsalkowski, from Warsaw. In later years Benny related his story to me concerning the German advance into Poland and his capture as a sixteen-year-old. He was forced to work in a German factory until his escape to England, where he promptly volunteered and returned to fight the Germans! He also told of how the Poles, fighting their way up the slopes of Monte Cassino, would get in front of the allies' 'creeping barrage' and, in their eagerness to get at the Germans dug in there, were blasted by their own guns! He had many stories about how he was brought up on a farm with his two brothers, Janeck (James) and Stanislaus (Stanley), was taken for forced labour by the Germans, and about shootings and internments - it was all so real.

Next to Benny was Reg Hawkins, ex-RAF fitter with whom, in times to come, I would talk of nothing else but Avro Lancasters, Lincolns and other bombers. There was big Roger Anderson, Paddy Meli, Harry Woolridge and Les Williams (who had just been demobbed from the Royal Corps of Signals Motorcycle Display Team and was later to become a key member of Doug Heles' team). After Les came Harry Wright, and across from him was the engine bench. This, as the name implies, dealt with the (pre-unit) engines alone. The legendary Jimmy Dalton - ex-Rudge racing mechanic and about 75 years old but so knowledgeable it was unbelievable - was closely followed by Bert Marlow, ex-Navy fitter who smoked a pipe (more about that later) and David Tandy. These were the three most senior engine benchmen and very experienced. The last person on the engine bench was George Cahill who, though quite young, was a competent and thorough person, slow and deliberate in his work. These were engine men who could build an engine from scratch and know, without it even turning, that it would be okay. Their job was the restoration of engine units alone — nothing else — whilst the fitters, mentioned earlier, were responsible for all aspects of machinery under warranty.

Towards the bottom of the repair shop were the Brown brothers, Ron and Ken. They dealt with the fork assemblies and spring wheels while, at the bottom of the shop, Jimmy Davis, ex-Fleet Air Arm, was in charge of the frame section. The man who repaired the petrol tanks, did the welding and so on, was Freddie Blomfield, a gruff, thickset man in his leather apron, who regularly lit his pipe with his oxyacetylene torch (there wasn't much pipe left, actually!) Before starting work on a petrol tank that needed repairing, the petroleum gas had to be obviated. We had a water tank for this purpose, where the petrol tanks were soaked for about 24 hours to rid them of the fumes. Freddie, however, had a different approach: he'd put the tank on his workbench and waft his oxy-torch across the open filler cap neck! There would be a low sort of 'whoomph' and that was it; now he could carry on. I often expected him to go up like a fiery comet, but he never did.

Then there were the labourers, important to the well-running of the shop. Arthur "Fag" Ashley (who, incidentally, married Tot, sister to Dave Tandy on the engine bench) rode a Speed Twin combo and lived at Eaves Green, a small gathering of cottages near Fillongley village. I remember one snowy morning when everything was a white-over, Arthur, combo and all slid into the ditch along the Fillongley to Meriden lane and three or four of us had to go and dig him out of the snowdrift in which he'd managed to bury himself. His partner was George Ellison, from Meriden village, who was in charge of the caustic vat. This was where the damaged items - mudguards, petrol tanks and so on - were stripped back to bare metal before going for repair. Arthur was also responsible for making the tea in the mornings and afternoons and bringing it round to each fitter, served in each individual's enamel mug. Arthur made a lovely cup of tea!

The road tester at this time was a small bespectacled chap called Les Millsom; an extremely knowledgeable man. He would go to the service counter when a customer arrived for an appointment, talk to him and get an idea of the complaint in question. Then, after putting his trade plates on the bike, take it for a test run. Upon returning to the repair shop he would make out his test report and from his findings the chargehand could make out the job card from which the fitter would carry out the required rectifications.

One of my favourite people in the department was a small, round, bald chap in brown overalls named David Pyot who, when I started there must have been all of 70 years of age! I think he was employed on what was called a green card, which allowed a person past the retirement age of 65 to carry on working, provided he was fit and able. He had completed almost 50 years at Triumph in one job or another and was the best chap I've ever seen at making control cables: it was David who taught me how to make cables correctly and solder nipples on properly so that they didn't pop off when the lever was pulled. This stood me in good stead as now, in later years, I make all my own cables for the bikes I restore.

Last, but not least, was the foreman's secretary, Kay Whittle. She did all the typing, made out the job cards from the test reports and generally kept the office in order. It seemed (to me, at least) that what Kay said carried a lot of weight, but it wasn't until a few weeks later that, sitting talking to Reg Hawkins during an afternoon tea-break, I discovered she was the sister of Frank Whittle, the man who invented the jet engine.

In later years, after Kay had left, I regretted not prevailing upon her good nature and asking more about her brother, who later became Sir Frank Whittle. Apparently, he carried out his pioneering work and initial experiments at Lutterworth, only a few miles from where I now live. In 1948 when I was about ten years old and still living in Coventry, I remember hearing the faint roar of jet engines being tested at Baginton on the other side of the city. I was aviation mad, (mainly thanks to my father who, during the war, was in the Navy on motor torpedo boats and brought home on leave a stack of aircraft recognition magazines for me). During the school holidays, I used to sit up a tree with a pair of old binoculars (my grandad's from the first war) and watch a Lancaster (or was it a Lincoln?) bomber which had one of its Merlin engines removed and a jet engine slung in its place. It would fly around all day, landing and taking off again, much to my delight.

Up in the roof of the repair shop we had a storage area: the design of factories in the 1940s and 1950s meant that the ridged roofs afforded a considerable amount of space. In the repair shop roof hung front and rear frames, front and rear mudguards and several other types of cycle parts. At the end of the shop was a rack affixed to the wall on which petrol tanks and front fork assemblies were kept. All these were service exchange items, in other words, if a chap had an accident on his bike — say, bent his forks and dented his petrol tank — he could take them along to his local dealer, who would bring them to the factory on dealers' day (Wednesday). They would be inspected by the chargehand, a job card made out and issued and then, together with the card, brought into the repair shop. Identical items would be found off the rack and supplied at a service exchange price (which was greatly reduced compared with that of a new item). The returned damaged items would then be put through the system, ending up on the rack ready to be used again!

With bent frames, the job card would be made out, noting year, model, frame number and so on. The frame would be given to Jimmy Davis, who selected an identical service exchange frame off the rack. The damaged frame's number would be stamped on to the exchange frame before it was handed back over the counter to the dealer. Jimmy would disc-off the number on the bent frame, after which it went for stripping back to bare metal in the caustic vat before being sent to Jack Clarke in the frame shop for straightening and rejigging. Next it would be Bonderised (an etching coat to key the paint to the bare metal), then on to the stove enamel shop for painting. Bob Cockburn would dip the frame in black stoving enamel and hang it up to proceed slowly through the oven for baking. When finished, it would end up back on the rack or hanging on a hook in the roof of the repair shop — a perfect job.

Many years later in 1983, when I was involved in the restoration of my own Tiger 100, the police had to examine the engine and frame numbers prior to the original registration number being reissued. As you will learn later on in the story, my Tiger 100 had been thrown down the road and wrapped around a telegraph pole, thus necessitating a replacement frame. After completing a total restoration in 1984 and '85, I made a request for the original

JRW 405 today, restored and in pristine condition, after a run to John Nelson's (ex service manager) home in Newark. Speed was 60-70mph on the A46 and petrol consumption just over 70mpg.

number but, before Swansea would reissue it, an examination had to be carried out by two experienced police officers to ensure that the bike was what I said it was.

They came along to my workshop and, after a lot of messing about with a file and emery-paper, uncovered the frame number — but, they also found the remnants of another number! The expression on the face of one of the young chaps was unbelievable; he honestly thought he'd found a 'knocked-off' bike. I couldn't convince them otherwise so looked out all my service exchange literature and told them of the procedure whereby frames for reconditioning had the numbers erased prior to re-enamelling. They were still not entirely convinced but, saying that they were going to have to seek expert assistance on this, they left (apparently, they had to contact someone to verify my story, possibly an expert on Triumphs). About ten days later, whilst I was busily working, a knock came on the workshop door and in walked the two policemen. Rather sheepishly, the younger of the two started to tell me of the procedures that they'd had to follow, whilst I made them both a cup of coffee. Apparently, after leaving me, they had reported the partially obliterated second number to their superior who decreed that the frame number was to be dissected to determine when it was originally stamped. I wasn't sure whether this was technically possible but was assured rather seriously that the Birmingham Police forensic laboratory could do anything, even down to dating a metal stamp (it didn't seem to occur to them that the frame would have to be cut through to do this). So, over coffee, and as politely as I could, I told them that under no circumstances was I going to let someone cut up my beloved JRW's front frame! Off they went again. Another week went by before they returned, even more sheepishly this time. By now I was marvelling at the time and expense expended on the issue. Over another cup of coffee, I asked, "OK, so what now?" and the younger one replied, "Well, Mr Hancox, we didn't know what to do so we asked our boss who told us to contact the Triumph Owners Club of Great Britain to see who could help on this. They referred us to you!" After another cup of coffee and handshakes all round, off they went, fairly contented, I think. Anyway, soon after my new V5 document came through bearing the registration number JRW 405, so at last I could tax the bike and get it on the road.

So, this was the repair shop in which I was to work under the guiding hand of Joe Bosworth and later on Reg Hawkins, both excellent tutors and good friends in years to come.

JRW 405

I suppose any young chap who works in an English motorcycle factory but doesn't ride one of the products comes in for a certain amount of stick. Having a 500cc Red Hunter Ariel, 1952 model (which was extremely quick as well as frugal on juice) was a good idea originally. When problems arose with the big end, however, a certain amount of ribbing was inevitable! With the aid of Reg Hawkins I fitted a new roller big end, trued the flywheels and fitted them back in the motor. Things ran okay for a while until, one night during tea, my father said, "I work with a chap who has a Tiger 100 for sale, £60 I think, do you want me to enquire?"

Well, after asking a certain Mr Fred Millard of 182 Burnaby Road, Coventry, it came to light that he had purchased the bike new from Brandish's, the main Triumph dealer in Coventry, ridden it for two years, then over-zealously tickled the carburettor one cold morning and set the bike on fire! After it had been rebuilt under the insurance at the service department, it went back to his house, where it remained untouched in his shed until the day I opened the door and gazed upon JRW 405 for the first time.

Boy-oh-boy, was she rough! Fred hadn't summoned up enough courage to attempt a start-up since the rebuild so it had stood, rusting, until the day I saw it. Apart from the chrome parts, rims, exhaust pipes, handlebars and levers, it was in super condition. The tyres were flat but a little air from my father's car tyre pump soon put that right! With a shaking hand I turned on the right-hand fuel tap, tickled the float until it flooded, turned the air lever to choke, freed the clutch and depressed the kickstarter. The engine fired at once and, after checking the oil return, pressure, and opening the choke, it settled down to the most silent and steady beat. I couldn't believe it: here was a bike that hadn't run for two years, ticking over as if it had been only yesterday it was despatched from Meriden. I handed over my £60 (hard-earned, borrowed, scraped-together cash) and, with my father following, rode home my newly-acquired Triumph twin.

The 1947 Victory Parade in London with Metropolitan Police riders mounted on 1947 Speed Twin models. The King (George VI) and Queen are taking the salute.

My first impression was that it was so light compared with the Ariel 500, almost tinny. The power was smoother and the motor very responsive and twitchy. After riding the Red Hunter with the Ariel trailing-link rear suspension, it felt as if the sprung hub wasn't working at all. I soon found out, however, from a quick look back and down that the sprung hub was working away quite merrily.

The next morning I duly turned up for work on the Tiger, parking it in the bike sheds, where it came in for a lot of good-natured jibes due to its rusty state. Some of the remarks must have got back to the foreman, Mr Fields, as he came to me during the

The author on JRW 405 at Kirkby Mallory. Note the chromed bottom fork legs and Trophy front guard, which was all the rage then.

Tales of Triumph & Meriden

The 1946-48 separate headlight arrangement commonly used by most postwar manufacturers.

morning and said he'd heard that I'd taken the sensible step and bought a Triumph. "Why don't you bring it into the shop at lunchtime so that we can look at it?" he said. Obviously, I couldn't wait for the lunchbreak bell to go. I sprinted down through the factory, got on my bike and, as nonchalantly as I could, rode it round to the repair shop doors. Upon entering, I was greeted by cheers and ribald remarks about its rusty condition. Mr Fields came and looked at the bike, remarking on this and that, in the end saying "Well, I suppose you'd better get it cleaned up, hadn't you?" Joe Bosworth nudged me and whispered, "That's it, son, you've got carte blanche!" I suppose I looked a bit blank so Joe nudged me again and said "Get it in at the bottom of the shop, get the wheels out and the exhaust system off." The spanners flew and, with Joe and Reg helping, a replacement exhaust, service exchange front wheel and new MkII sprung hub were fitted in an amazingly rapid time. With the new parts the bike looked 100 per cent better, but the kickstart, gearchange lever, handlebars and accompanying parts were still rusty. Never mind, these would be substituted over the ensuing weeks until my beautiful JRW 405 was immaculate! If ever there was a chap who worshipped a bike, I guess it was me!

I knew my call-up date was looming and I wanted to get the Tiger in tip-top condition in case it was needed.

It was about this time that I again met my future wife, Gloria, whom I'd originally courted for a short time until her mother put a stop to her seeing "that motorcycling ruffian." I'd always known that I'd get back to seeing her again but how and when, I guess I didn't know. I had a good friend at the time called Barrie Ratcliffe who rode an extremely quick T110 as if there was no tomorrow! Barrie and I went on holiday to Cornwall for a fortnight, spent a lovely fourteen days in and around Penzance and, during that time, I sent two postcards to Gloria: I couldn't get her out of my mind.

It was also exactly the time when Barrie and I discovered we had to register for National Service. We were walking up Market Jew Street in Penzance when Barrie stopped dead in his tracks and said under his breath, "Bloody hell." I turned to see where he was looking and, to my horror, found myself staring at a poster in the window of the GPO which said "All male persons born between the dates ...." Well, that was it. Doom and gloom for the remainder of the holiday, with the realisation that as soon as we got back to Coventry we had to go and register ourselves for National Service. The holiday all too soon came to an end and, after saying cheerio to some of our new friends (local lads who owned and rode Triumphs), we set off on the long trek home.

The 1949 Tiger 100, with Alex Scobie showing off the new model with streamlined headlight enclosure.

We went to the Department of Employment in Coventry to register where,

THE unprecedented popularity of Triumph multi-cylinder motor cycles since the end of World War II is a fitting reward for the bold policy introduced of scrapping the military type single-cylinder machines which, successful as they were in the war, were thought to be inadequate for the new peace era.

For 1949 we continue to offer a beautifully-made twin-cylinder range with a number of notable improvements which, notwithstanding the many difficulties faced by post-war Britain, are an indication to the world of the progressive policy pursued by this Company in its determination to maintain, by merit, the foremost position Triumph holds today.

Discriminating motor cyclists and sportsmen throughout the world can be assured that their enthusiasm is matched by a group of workpeople engaged in the manufacture of what we believe to be the best motor cycle in the world, and we look forward with confidence to the continuance of their support in the future.

The standard roadster range comprises three models :—

349 c.c. 3T de LUXE : 498 c.c. SPEED TWIN : 498 c.c. TIGER 100

Details of Road Racing and Trials machines may be obtained on application.

TRIUMPH ENGINEERING COMPANY LIMITED,
Telephone : COVENTRY 60221

The 1949 catalogue cover was rather subdued, especially as it heralded the introduction of the famous nacelle fully enclosed headlight.

to make it even worse, Barrie got a deferment as he was an indentured apprentice at Dunlop Aviation on the Holbrooks Lane in Coventry. No such luck for me, a seven-year traineeship didn't count, so, a few weeks later, I went to Highfield House on the Tamworth Road, just outside Coventry (one of the area health centres) for my medical. That was a joke, if ever I saw one. As long as you could walk you were in! I suppose the medics were wise to just about every trick in the book, so I didn't even bother to say "Sorry I didn't hear you" or "Isn't it a bit dark in here?" One of the chaps who sat in the queue outside reckoned he'd been told by an old sweat that if you ate a pinch of cordite out of a bullet it turned your face grey and your eyes red — which might get you off the hook! Sitting naked, except for our shorts, outside some bloke's office, I thought "Great, where do we get a bullet from?" We went through the usual tests: eyes, ears, look in your mouth, up your nose, a resounding tap on each side of the chest, a whack on the knees and elbows with a rubber mallet, then after drop 'em and cough, it was "Okay, son, A1." God, that was it, I was in. Getting dressed with a heavy heart and a terrible sense of foreboding, I rode JRW home as if the end of the world was just around the corner ...

Using my impending call-up as an excuse, I plucked up courage to call Gloria the following Saturday and ask her out for a date — on the Tiger 100, of course.

Having notified the factory that Her Majesty would be requiring my services on May 23 and thereafter, all I could do was wait and make the best of what time was left to me. It all came to a head one night when I came home from work. Entering the kitchen

after putting away JRW, I was met with a funny silence from both Mum and Dad. It wasn't until I looked at the table that I saw propped against my teacup and saucer a buff-coloured envelope marked OHMS. I opened it with trembling hands and a hollow feeing inside. It didn't seem that long since I'd started at Meriden; just a couple of short years to get into the swing of things, make friends and get to belong to one of the best bunch of workmates a chap could ask for and acquire a smashing girlfriend as well. The letter simply said "You will present yourself at Catterick Garrison on such and such a day at such and such a time"; no "If you've nothing better to do" or "please" in sight! There was a one-way rail warrant from Coventry to Richmond and that, in itself, seemed to underline the finality of it all. So, that was it.

At work, over the last couple of months I was given all sorts of advice from both Reg Hawkins and Les Williams, but nothing registered, really; I was wandering around as if in a trance. The only two things that really mattered were Glo (my nickname for Gloria) and JRW 405. However, after a couple of days I seemed to resign myself to the inevitable and things definitely started to appear brighter. After all, I thought to myself "It's only two years." Two years, or 24 months, or 104 weeks, or 730 days: it didn't really sound that long, did it?

High jinks

Back at the start of my time at Meriden, Joe Bosworth had been a fitter extraordinaire, a fearsome character and my initial tutor. He wasn't above giving me a smack on the back of the head if I didn't do what he wanted quickly enough or in the right way.

The first bike I ever worked on with Joe was a 1953 sprung hub Speed Twin with AC lighting and ignition systems. This was the very first coil ignition twin, having separate lighting and ignition switches, with a one-and-a-half inch diameter ammeter mounted just above them and below the speedometer — all in the nacelle top. The amount of wiring required for this first AC system earned it the nickname the Battersea Power Station! The huge three-penny bit shaped alternator, housed in the primary chaincase, meant that the case itself had to be redesigned and increased in frontal area to accommodate the thing.

It also meant that the engine shaft shock absorber was no longer able to be used on the drive side of the engine, as the rotor for the alternator was there in its place. There had to be some sort of shock absorbing system in the primary drive, so logic dictated it should be at the opposite end in the clutch itself. When we young chaps, with bikes that had the original engine shaft shock absorber with the big cush-drive spring, saw the new clutch we thought "Aha, if we fit this to our own bikes, together with what we already have, we'll end up with a super smooth transmission and, as an added bonus, extra life on the primary chain!"

This theory was later proven, as I found during my two years' Army service. When I could get weekend passes, I'd belt JRW the 148 miles home from Yorkshire to Coventry by Saturday lunchtime, and then return to Yorkshire late on Sunday night, usually arriving back at camp in Ripon in the early hours of Monday morning. This just gave me time for a couple of hour's sleep before reveille, but not enough time to check over the Tiger for the next week's run! This went on and on and on, weekend after weekend, and I don't think I ever had to adjust the chains!

PERFORMANCE

STAMINA

QUALITY

The 1950 brochure.

One of the problems with the new AC system, introduced in 1953 on the Speed Twin only and then, in 1954, on the 6T Thunderbird, was the huge rectangular rectifier mounted beneath the saddle and its accompanying resistor. This was an asbestos strip, mounted on insulated brackets and wire-wound and its job was to dissipate excess current by converting it into heat. Sometimes, therefore, if you looked at one of the things in poor light they actually glowed. We nicknamed this set-up the 'toast-rack.' Due to lots of failures of the Lucas AC system under warranty, which dealers couldn't sort out as it was so new, the bikes were returned to the Triumph service repair shop for rectification.

As the problems grew more intense — and sometimes even we couldn't solve them permanently — Lucas sent a couple of service engineers to help. From this liaison was born the later system, using the single PRS8 lighting and ignition switch (making room in the nacelle top for the 2 inch ammeter used on the magneto model Tigers). It also meant that lighting and ignition circuitry - and the actual loom - could be abbreviated, making more room inside the nacelle behind the headlight unit. The final improvement was to remove the large rectangular rectifier and asbestos toast rack, replacing both with the new round shaped rectifier introduced at the same time.

These two brochure covers of 1951 (right) and 1952 (above) epitomise the carefree days of motorcycling and shows off to perfection the beautifully streamlined-looking Twins.

This was my first actual job with Joe, changing a Speed Twin over to the new system (which also meant replacing the nacelle top with one with appropriate holes for the changed instruments and switches. They say your first experience of anything always makes a lasting impression and I suppose this is why now, after all these years, I can still put together a nice sprung hub Speed Twin or Tiger 100.

One of the more unusual bikes I

was required to work on with Joe was a 1954 iron-engined Tiger 110 owned by an eccentric millionaire. We knew him as Mr Palethorpe and found out, subsequently, that he was the original Mr Palethorpe of Palethorpe sausages! He had worked on the new bike himself and carried out quite a few non-standard modifications which included fitting dropped Grand Prix type bars as supplied in the high performance racing kit of the day. But these were fitted upside down, putting the twistgrip reduced end on the left-hand side, which meant that, not only was the Triumph-patented twistgrip on the wrong side of the handlebars when you were seated on the bike, but to open the throttle you had to roll the grip away from you!

You may well think this alteration was bad enough, but Mr Palethorpe had also moved the clutch lever and fitted it on the right-hand side where you would normally expect the front brake to be. From the top of the first bend on each exhaust pipe, he had welded adaptors to accept flexible pipes, the ends of which were joined to the handlebar ends, thus heating the bars and grips for cold weather riding! We just couldn't believe it, but it was true all the same and a hell of a nightmare to ride, as Bozzy (Joe) found out to his cost. The beautiful twin seat had been removed and replaced with what can only be described as a wooden cowboy saddle covered in sacking! All this on a nearly-new Tiger 110.

To make matters worse, the bike had to be tested after whatever work that was required had been carried out and Les Milsom, the tester, can still be seen in my mind's eye, standing adamant, arms akimbo, slowly shaking his head and muttering "Not bloody likely!" That's how Bozzy came to grief, bravely stepping in and saying "I'll whizz it up and down the drive — surely that'll be enough!" We all looked on in apprehension, knowing that Joe was a brave bloke, but it wasn't enough, as he was about to find out.

After several attempts to move off in first gear — starting up and pulling in the right-handed clutch to engage gear wasn't a problem, but letting out the clutch and trying to increase revs by the left-handed, reverse-operation twistgrip was - and amidst well-meant snatches of advice from us all, Joe erratically wobbled out through the rubber swing door and on to the concrete drive. At this point, if I had been riding I would have stopped and tried to focus my mind again before attempting anything else, but not Bozzy 'Bull-at-a-gate' Joe. Straight off down the drive with plenty of left-hand, backward throttle. We could sense what was coming next: with a big flourish, confident he had mastered the beast, Joe attempted a quick change up into second gear. Whether he suffered a mental block that instant, we don't know, but, instead of de-clutching, he slapped on the front brake with disastrous consequences: the 8inch front brake locked the wheel and it was all over in an instant, with Joe and the bike in a big heap.

After getting the bike back up on the bench, I started replacing the scratched, dented and bent items, whilst Joe went to surgery to have his cuts and grazes dressed and bandaged. A decision to put the controls back to standard for testing purposes was made by the foreman, Mr Fields, much to Les Milsom's relief who, after he'd taken a quick spin on it, declared the bike okay to be returned to its owner. We opted to leave the controls as standard because a little while later a telephone call came in to the service department from Mr Palethorpe asking if we could deliver the bike to his Birmingham home.

Later on in the day, Les Milsom rode the bike to the customer's house and was collected by Albert Charlton, the chargehand, in his car and brought back

TRIUMPH

The Best Motorcycle in the World

Another 1951 brochure cover shows how Triumph motorcycles were used in the world of trials riding and road racing.

to the factory. It was their story and description of the ramshackle, overgrown mansion where Mr Palethorpe lived that held our attention the most. Halfway along his drive was an abandoned Rolls-Royce, on flat tyres and with grass growing up through the floorboards; apparently it had run out of petrol and that's exactly where it had stopped rolling! He'd never bothered with it since. I often wonder what happened to that very odd new Triumph Tiger 110 that spat Bozzy off unceremoniously down the back drive.

For the first year of production the swinging-arm Tiger 100s and Tiger 110s did not have sidecar fixing points, as Edward Turner didn't want people fitting sidecars to his new frames. 1954 was the only year that we built bikes in both rigid and swinging-arm frame guises! Edward Turner decided that the Speed Twin and Thunderbird models would continue be made as they were, equipped with the MkII spring wheel, which, after all, was really good for sidecar work. Therefore, if anyone wanted a sidecar bike, it had to be a 5T or 6T, but if you wanted a sports solo, then the high performance swinging-arm framed Tigers were the ticket.

It's a good job, really, because the new models started coming in with

Tales of Triumph & Meriden

fractured rear frame stays (the rear frame stays descend from the top rear suspension fixing points to the rear of the gearbox on the offside and to the rear of the primary chaincase on the rearside). To these stays are affixed (by brazing) the castings which are threaded and take the triangular plates, on to which are hung the silencer and pillion footrest assemblies. Whether it was because the silencers waggled which, in turn, stressed the brazed on fixing lug I don't know, but the frame tubes cracked through immediately above the lug, thus necessitating a frame change under warranty. The remedy was to pass an instruction down to the frame shop that before the lug was brazed on, a stiffening steel shoe, slightly longer than the lug, was welded to the tube. The lug was then brazed to the shoe which acted as a reinforcement. To cut down on the waggle, sway-braces were affixed to the pipe to silencer clips and from there inwards to a central stud fixing below the swinging-arm. After these measures were introduced, we had no more breakages.

It really did seem simple, back in those days, to rectify a fault, unlike later on when goodness knows how many people were involved and nothing happened for weeks, sometimes months!

A rear-frame change was usually accomplished quite easily within the day appointment system with two fitters working one each side of the bike. The exhaust system, rear wheel, twin seat, rear mudguard, battery box and oil tank were removed. After the rear chainguard and suspension units were taken off, the primary chaincase and complete transmission was removed. This now allowed access to the bottom gearbox pivot bolt and the bottom rear engine gearbox plate through bolt. The top saddle tube, front to rear frame stud and front down tube bottom through stud (which holds the two frames together at that point) were the last to undo and remove so that the rear frame could be detached. It really was an easily completed, within-the-working-day, operation, far easier than what was to come later on in 1971 ...

The months passed so quickly working there; you were amongst good chaps who were always willing to help and point out the error of your ways (sometimes with the toe of their boot!) but lessons were generally learnt well and, by the time my call-up date came on May 23, I was competent and quite capable of carrying out most operations on my own with light supervision from Joe.

To give me a wider and more varied view of the repair shop for my last few months I was taken from Joe and put with Reg Hawkins, a good man on Tiger Cubs. Reg was about 40 years old then, so he was a lot older than me but not quite so big in stature. What he lacked in size, however, was made up for in temper: on more than one occasion my reactions had to be razor-sharp to dodge flying spanners or anything else that came quickly to hand if I had done something wrong.

As young Les Williams was more my age, he and I would often fool about, usually getting a telling-off for something or other. On one particular occasion Reg had left me to change a rear wheel under warranty (something to do with poor chrome on the rim, I think). I removed the wheel whilst Reg got on with the other problems with the engine (at this time -1956 - Tiger Cubs suffered from excessive timing gear noise and carburettor problems). Much to his annoyance, Les and myself were carrying on with some sort of argument and gradually his temper boiled over. After telling us both to pipe down he went to the stores counter to hand in the spares requisition he'd made out for the replacement parts. I'd got the bike's wheel out and removed the brake plate, brake shoes and the tyre and tube and, by now, our argument had progressed to throwing things at each other (silly, I know, but we were young). Just then something hit me on the backside. Les had cut two rings of rubber from an old tube, knotted them together, double knotted them again and shot me with it. By crikey, it stung like the blazes and quick as a flash I threw a tyre lever at him, which missed, thankfully. Just as he threw it back, Reg saw us and shouted, which distracted my attention somewhat. I heard the tyre lever bounce, but couldn't find it. Reg handed me the new rear wheel and then, when my hands were full, smacked me on the back of the head with his knuckles, and that smarted as well! Willie (Les) was, by now, in hysterics, but I thought I'd better play safe and get on with some work. First job was to put the tyre and tube on, but being short of one of Reg's tyre levers didn't prevent that so I thought I'd look for the missing lever later on when the job was finished; after all, the customer was waiting in reception to ride his bike home.

A little while saw the job completed and tested, with only the newly rebuilt carburettor to be finally set and I still hadn't found the tyre lever! About an hour later, the first pangs of doubt began to creep into my mind. I asked Les at which angle he'd thrown the thing: had he seen where it bounced? No, he hadn't. I was about to say something to Reg when Mr Fields came out of his office and shouted Reg to go and see him. Mumbling that "This always happens at going-home time" (it was 5.05 and we knocked off at 5.15pm), Reg marched swiftly up the workshop. By this time I'd got my Barbour suit bottoms and riding boots on and, as I was struggling into my jacket, I looked towards the office. Reg was standing in front of Mr Fields' desk and, from the expression on his face, I could see that he wasn't pleased at all. After Mr Fields had finished, Reg turned on his heel and, with a face the colour of beetroot, came down the repair shop — straight for me. I could tell from his look he meant business, so I grabbed my helmet and started to edge around to the other side of the trestle. He tried to grab me but I moved back out of his reach saying "What's up Reg?" as innocently as I could. "What's up, what's bloody up?" he hissed "I'll tell you what's up. That sodding customer had a rear wheel puncture on the way home and guess what he found inside his rear tyre?" I thought "Oh sugar, that's where it went!" Reg went on, "As if that wasn't bad enough, the tyre lever had my bloody name on it!" How I got away with it I'll never know, but Reg took that telling off for me and for that I'll always be grateful.

I remember that about this time, towards the end of 1955, a great wave of euphoria swept through the factory when we learned that a young Texan named Johnny Allen had ridden a streamlined Thunderbird across the Bonneville Salt Flats and set a new world speed record of 193mph. We knew the old iron-engined 6T was good, but not that good! When the streamlined projectile was brought over to the factory later on, we all had a good chance to look it over and I think everyone came to the conclusion that this guy was really brave to ride this aluminium cigar capsule at those speeds. Once should have been enough, but immediately he'd set the 193mph record, NSU went out and broke it on a works-prepared, supercharged 500cc streamliner at 211mph. Not to be outdone, the brave, slightly-built Allen, with the experience and backing of tuner Jack Wilson, promptly went back to Bonneville and pushed the record up to 214mph. This really upset the German NSU team which had, amidst a great splurge of publicity, returned home saying it had beaten the 650 Triumph with a 500.

Tales of Triumph & Meriden

After all the fuss had died down, we learned of a major disappointment concerning the second attempt; it wasn't to be ratified as there wasn't an FIM official present at the attempt. Although everyone present agreed that things were all above board with regard to the timing of the runs, witnesses and so on, as an official FIM observer was not present the record wasn't recognized. It didn't matter to us, though, everyone at Meriden knew and that gave us an enormous lift.

When the Johnny Allen record-breaker bike came over to England it arrived at Elmdon (Birmingham International, as it is now) airport on a Douglas DC3 Dakota and, after unloading was brought the short way to Meriden on the back of the work's lorry. It was quite a day: I remember the streamliner on its stands, reposing in the main finishing shop where everyone could have a chance to see it and, of course, Johnny Allen who must have lost his voice and the use of his right-hand throughout the day. I seem to recollect that, some days later, the publicity department had the projectile taken over to Gaydon airfield for some photographic stint, but whether the streamliner was fired up and ridden past the cameras I don't recall. It all ended well that week, and after a civic reception in Coventry, the young Texan returned to America, a hero in the eyes of us all.

Back in the repair shop, Willie was about to pull another of his tricks on any unsuspecting person he could find and I watched him intently so as to learn his crafty art. He held out his open hand to me palm upwards and there nestling in it was a glistening new gudgeon pin circlip. He looked at me and gave a slow wink. It was now almost half past three in the afternoon, and anyone who had been given a major engine job on the day appointment system would be just about finishing off and almost ready to refit the petrol tank prior to starting up the motor for the first time. You must remember, we were very proud of the fact that we were the only motorcycle factory repair department in the world who offered this unique service, whereby a customer could arrive at 8.30 in the morning and by 4.30 in the afternoon ride home on his machine, which had been subjected to a thorough overhaul of the engine and transmission. A fitter who had carried out such a speedy and efficient task was full of self-satisfaction when the job was nearing completion and would be whistling as he wiped down the workbench and put his tools away in their allotted places.

It was precisely at this moment that the dreaded Willie struck! Whilst the fitter had his back turned, Willie would saunter up the repair shop, past the end of the workbench and, quick as a flash, drop the circlip on the work surface where the engine components had lain in their dismantled state. All we had to do now was watch and wait. The chosen victim would still be whistling as he wiped the bench, prior to getting up on it to kickstart the bike, when his eyes would alight on the circlip laying there so innocently. This was the part we liked best; the whistling would stop instantly and you could see the torment as the fitter tried to remember whether he'd replaced both circlips before lowering the cylinder barrel over the pistons — or had he forgotten and fitted only one? The indecision came next; should he chance it, as the customer was waiting in reception to ride his newly overhauled bike home? He'd never have enough time to slip the top off the motor and check before going-home time — more mental wrestling — what to do, what to do? By this time, Willie was usually in fits and I was in awe of his nerve.

As the luckless victim finally gave in and reached for the spanners he'd just carefully wiped and put away, Willie would walk up and casually ask "Have you picked up a circlip of mine, I think I dropped it somewhere along here?" The intense look of relief was immediately followed by a curse or an oath as the penny dropped. Uncomplimentary phrases like "You bloody Welsh mountain goat — I'll get you, never fear!" were just so much water off a duck's back as far as Willie was concerned because he never did change — you always had to be on your guard, especially when he was on the prowl and looking for a target.

The Best Motorcycle in the World

Angels

There was, of course, a more mundane side to our days, where work progressed quickly and efficiently in order to get the customer back on the road. Our aim was to please the customer, attend to the problems and, by doing so quickly and efficiently, ensure that when and if he chose another bike, it would be a Triumph.

One of the best moments for Reg Hawkins and I came in the summer of 1956. Reg was a combination rider, owning a 1939 Tiger 100 with a single seat sidecar. (I'll always remember the registration number: GKP 15). There's no denying we were a jolly good team together, him working on one side of a bike and me on the other. I don't know when the SOS phone call came in but the day was bright and sunny and Reg and I were told to take the works general runabout van and go to the south-east of Coventry along the old A45 to rescue a family which had broken down on a Triumph motor bike and sidecar.

We didn't do this sort of thing very often, so it was something of an experience for me. It turned out the family was taking annual holidays, travelling from place to place on a planned itinerary, with two small children and all their luggage. The Thunderbird (a 1954 sprung hub model) was loaded with Mum, Dad, two kids and the luggage, something it nevertheless should have taken in its stride. Due to an error in servicing, however, whether in ignition timing or carburation, with a horrible noise the motor had packed in quite suddenly after a long pull up a gradient. As the owners were not a million miles away from Meriden, they decided it seemed an excellent opportunity to get the relatively new bike repaired expertly. They had resigned themselves to the fact that as this was only the second day, their holiday was now ruined. Reg loaded the Mum, kids and cases into the van whilst I attached the tow rope to the front of the sidecar chassis and, with Dad on the combo, off we set back to Meriden at a leisurely pace.

When we got to the repair shop, Merle Dawson, the manager's secretary, came out and escorted the family down to the canteen for something to eat and drink, whilst Reg and I set to work. In the 'outside place', as we used to call it (where the degreaser was housed), we set to and had the chair off in record time. We could now put the bike up on to the work trestle and find out what the problem was. It didn't take many minutes to discover that one piston had virtually disintegrated due to prolonged running at too high cylinder temperatures. The bits of aluminium from the piston had gone round the motor, thus necessitating a complete engine strip and rebuild.

Reg and I started, and I reckon we broke some sort of record that day.

TRIUMPH TIGER '100'
500 c.c. O.H.V. TWIN

Whether it was just a feeling we'd got or whether it was to try and salvage the family's holiday, I don't know, but we were inspired! Without even speaking to each other we removed the engine, dismantled it (including the crank), cleaned it all out and, each of us doing separate work so as to not double-up on the labour, we rebuilt the motor with new barrel and pistons, big ends, mains and anything else that had been contaminated by the aluminium debris. By late afternoon, (teabreak time, which was 3.50pm) we had the motor in and running.

It went out on test and, after minor rectifications, the sidecar was quickly refitted. A simple task really: just offer it up to the bike, locate the rear ball-joint and tighten, then front fitting, or the swan neck, as it was called, finally pushing the bolts through the saddle point and fourth point eyes. Everything was then tightened and, after connecting the sidecar light wire, the job was done.

Reg took the combo outside, started it up and rode it round to the front of

The 1940 Tiger 100, identical to GKP 15 owned and ridden by Reg Hawkins.

the service department and down the drive to the service reception steps. I guess the chap must have heard it because he came out of reception and just stood with his mouth open. Although the bike was strictly out of warranty, I think his bill was waived because of circumstances prevailing and, besides, he'd only got enough money for his holiday on him and we didn't want to spoil that, especially after our efforts! It didn't take long for him to get his family aboard, and amidst cheery waves and good wishes, off they went to continue their holiday after losing only a few hours. Reg and I looked at each other and smiled, a smile that said "Well done, mate." With that, in we went to clean up, wash and degrease the tools and clean down the bench, because by this time it was approaching going-home time and we wanted to be ready for the next day.

Neither of us thought any more about the episode until Mr Fields came to the workshop two weeks later carrying a copy of *Motorcycling* (or the *Green 'Un*, as it was called then). "You two chaps have got a mention!" he said with a smile, handing over the magazine to Reg. With me looking over his shoulder, we read, to our amazement, the glowing tribute to the Triumph service repair shop, the standard of work and especially the two chaps who had enabled the family to continue and enjoy its holiday. The piece finished off by saying "I've never met angels before, but, when and if I do, I bet they'll be wearing blue overalls!"

We have
ignition!

Returning to Tiger Cub faults (noisy timing gears and faulty carburation), by this time we had gone from the early Amal, with the separate mixing chamber/float bowl, to the horrible little Zenith MX (which, in the eyes of some of the fitters, was neither useful nor ornamental). I've never understood why Triumph always messed about and changed things that were perfectly okay and ignored things that really did want changing or modifying.

Oh well, enough of that. One other little bug-bear on the Cub of 1956 was the gear indicator housed in the nacelle top. This little gadget was cable-operated from the gearbox camplate, with the other end of the cable hooked up to a ratchet and pinion affair. It was secured into the nacelle top by two 5BA screws and had a dial face with a small pointer on it which read 1st-N-2nd-3rd-4th. When the gear pedal was depressed for first gear engagement, the camplate moved, operating the cable, which in turn operated the rack and pinion and moved the pointer to 1st on the dial. Moving the gear pedal into neutral, 2nd, 3rd or 4th didn't always correspond with what was on the dial, so adjustments to the mechanism were required. We fitters considered the gear indicator a waste of space and were of the opinion that if a rider didn't know what gear he was in without having to look at the 'idiot' indicator, as we called it, then he shouldn't be riding.

Anyway, on this fateful day, Reg was attending to the carburettor (changing jets to compensate for massive flat spots during what was laughingly called acceleration), whilst I stood on the bench with the headlight assembly out of the nacelle, attending to the indicator assembly. It was a bit of a fiddly operation, working inside the nacelle (I rather think that's why I got it) but, never mind, it was enjoyable just to be working there, no matter what the job.

Reg finished the carburettor and moved straight on to the noisy timing gear job. Now, to get to the timing gears on the Tiger Cub it's necessary to first of all remove the outer timing cover, gearchange and kickstart levers, providing access to the inner cover which housed bushes for the camshaft assembly. This

Tales of Triumph & Meriden

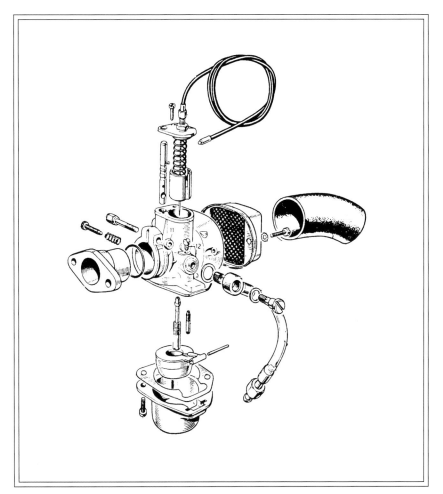

The little Zenith carburettor that caused so many problems and headaches with starting and running difficulties. It didn't stay around long and was soon replaced with the similar Amal.

assembly comprised the camshaft (on to which was keyed the main camwheel); the clutch-arm (from which you had to disconnect the clutch cable) and, finally, the camplate spindle, which was hidden behind a rectangular cover held on to the inner case by two countersunk cross-head screws. Once this cover was off you could, with a pair of pointed-nose pliers, remove the spindle split pin, pull out the spindle and then, when the cover screws around the inner timing case cover were taken out, the cover could be pulled off. You were now looking at the gear clusters in the gearbox and forward of that, housed in a separate compartment, the timing gears. In a smaller compartment below these was the oil pump, but this didn't figure in the camwheel change operation, so it was left alone.

I was making slow work of the gear indicator job; I just couldn't get the cable to curl around inside the nacelle and sit right. Reg had got all the timing

We have ignition!

The Terrier 150 was styled on the bigger Twins and, although small, had a big bike feel. It was introduced in 1954 with a publicity stunt called the 'Gaffer's Gallup' which entailed Edward Turner, Bob Fearon and A St J Masters riding three Terriers from Lands End to John O'Groats.

side off and had deftly slid out the camshaft and camwheel assembly, first of all turning the motor over to top dead centre on compression stroke so as to relieve any spring tension on the cam followers; then quickly, before they could overcome the oil suction and fall with gravity, replace it with an old camshaft, just to keep things in place. The next stage for him was to undo the engine distributor pinion centre bolt, which is a normal 5/16 inch bolt through the pinion that threads through the timing side flywheel shaft.

We all had our T-spanners, as they were called, and, by sliding the tommy-bar handle completely one way, you could, with a sharp tap from a hide mal-

Tales of Triumph & Meriden

let, undo the bolt, using the engine compression to prevent the engine from turning. As the bolt had a normal right-hand thread, this meant smacking the spanner anti-clockwise to undo and clockwise to re-tighten after the pinion had been replaced. We now arrive at the crucial point. I honestly didn't know that during my fiddling inside and around the nacelle top, I had inadvertently switched on the ignition! Reg had spun up the bolt and taking his hide mallet, gave the T-spanner a smack to tighten it. Of course, the engine fired and whipped the spanner round, giving Reg's knuckles a crack with the spanner tommy-bar. Needless to say, I was off and running through mid-air, before my feet even touched the ground. The hide mallet flew past me and then I heard his footsteps behind me, too, so I headed straight through the rubber swing doors at the bottom of the repair shop and out along the concrete drive down to the back of the factory as fast as I could.

The Tiger Cub nacelle and a clear view of the gear 'idiot' indicator and Lucas PRS8 lighting and ignition switch. The lightweight Cub was noted for its clean, uncluttered controls.

Drive-side view showing the clean and uncluttered lines of the Tiger Cub with the all-important cable runs so important to E.T. in publicity photographs.

You know how it is sometimes, when something tickles you and you can't do anything for laughing. This is how I was, stumbling, laughing, all the time fearful he would catch me. Normally I would easily have outpaced him, but he was a pretty nimble forty-year-old and I couldn't do anything for laughing. I ran, and ran, and all the time I could hear him behind me. I dared not stop and try to reason with him — he'd have killed me! I kept going and finally dared to look round: he was doubled over, hands on knees, gasping for breath. I started to walk back towards him; I knew I was risking a clout, but I couldn't help laughing. He slowly raised his head and looked at me with a very jaundiced eye, saying "If you ever do that again I'll bloody do you!" Then he grinned and we walked back to the workshop to get on with the Cub. I disconnected the battery on every one we reworked after that.

Later on that week we had word that Edward Turner was bringing his new wife down to the shop floor so that he could show her his domain. Edward Turner, or ET as we called him (before the Steven Spielberg one!) used to appear on the shop floor, going walkabout to see how things were. You hoped and prayed that this little man, with his piercing piggy eyes and Saville Row suit, didn't stop and look over your shoulder, for it was no good trying to bluff it if you couldn't do the job — because he could.

This particular day we got word that the service repair shop was to receive a visit from the great man, so we were ordered to do a real clean-up job; no stuff (engine parts or whatever) on the floor under your workbench (he was obsessed with that). We all had to clean down our own workbenches and finally, just before his arrival, take off our dirty overalls and slip on some new clean ones. We wondered at what point we should put on our new ones, but we needn't have worried because the chargehand came scooting round the corner into the shop, his arms waving and his eyes rolling, shouting "He's here, he's here!" We all quickly struggled into our new overalls and stood to attention, the chargehand and foreman doing the same outside their office. We stood for what seemed to be ages before we heard voices, then the unmistakable tones of Alec Masters, the service manager, who was escorting ET and his wife (who, I seem to recall, was some sort of beauty queen and Australian, but I'm not too sure on the latter) to the repair shop. They walked slowly down the shop whilst Alec Masters pointed out various things, then turned and walked back up again. I thought to myself "Please don't let him stop and ask questions." Thankfully, he didn't and we all struggled out of our new overalls, giving them to Arthur the labourer, put on our dirty ones and got on with some work. That was my first sighting of Edward Turner, the Main Man, or simply ET.

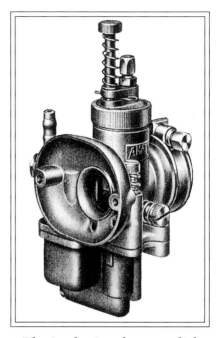

The Amal 32/1 carburettor which replaced the Zenith. It was a much-improved instrument which made the Tiger Cub much nicer to ride, and machines frequently gave over 100mpg using it.

The offending bolt, holding the engine pinion onto the crankshaft. Repair shop fitters favoured tightening it by hitting against compression with a Britool T-spanner, but not with the ignition on!

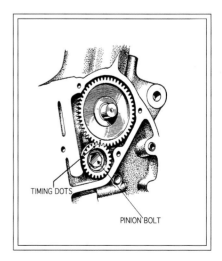

TIMING DOTS

PINION BOLT

Travellers

One job that needed to do done quickly was the rebuilding of a 1956 Speed Twin which was ridden overland to England by two Indian chaps all the way from that continent. As the job absolutely had to be concluded within two and a half days, Reg and I were instructed to "just dismantle and rebuild it completely, using service exchange tinware. It's got to look new and be new inside." This was a joint order from both the service manager and publicity department, then under the guiding force of Mr Ivor Davies.

The bike, as you might imagine on a journey such as that, had sustained awful damage to the cycle parts (frame, forks, wheels, mudguards and petrol tank). Before starting off from India, a huge pair of panniers had been fabricated to accommodate all the Indians' belongings, and these were fixed to either side of the rear mudguard. I'd never seen such big boxes on a bike: "It must steer like a drunken camel" I thought to myself, looking at the monsters.

The two chaps, one quite large and chubby, the other slim and rather military, were cheerful souls, with huge smiles and brilliant white teeth. The account of their journey was hair-raising to say the least, as neither of them could be called experienced motorcyclists.

Reg and I worked quite hard and eventually got this tired old Speed Twin back into pristine condition, much to the Indians' delight. We all stood and posed for an official photograph, with one or two of the other repair shop chaps getting in on it. After it had been tested and rectifications done, we said cheerio to the Indians outside the service department (at the bottom of the steps, actually), and off they rode into the sunset.

We used to find that people who made these horrendous journeys back in the mid-fifties were usually academics who were not experienced riders! The experienced chaps would look at a trip like that and probably say "No, thank you."

Another such inexperienced journeyman was Anthony Smith, journalist, broadcaster and, in later years, a good friend. Anthony had gone to South

Two travellers who had ridden overland from India in 1955, had their Speed Twin refurbished in Meriden service repair department before riding home again. A young author is second from the right.

Africa for some reason in 1954, and whilst in Cape Town espied a motorcycle shop in Waterkant Street. In this shop was a nearly-new 1955 plunger rear suspension Tiger Cub (Anthony admitted to me in later years that it was the lovely blue colour of the bike which caught his eye!) Not knowing A from a bull's foot, he got someone to make carrying-frames from angle iron and had them attached to the back of the little bike (and Anthony is about 6 foot 4 inches tall). Next, he purchased a stout English sports jacket, a pair of goggles, a pair of gauntlets and a beret, and set off on his newly-acquired purchase, learning as he went. They say ignorance is bliss and Anthony proceeded to ride the 7000 miles straight up Africa, going over deserts where he had to walk through deep sand alongside his little bike whilst it pulled along in first gear, and through wild bush. If you ever come across a book called *High Street Africa* it's the complete account of Anthony Smith's epic journey and well worth a read.

When he arrived back in England in 1956, Anthony contacted Meriden and, of course, we were only too pleased to have the little bike back for re-

Tales of Triumph & Meriden

The 1956 Tiger Cub with 'plunger' rear frame and 16 inch diameter wheels (Blue Sheen painted rim centre and lined black). The space under the twin seat included a valance which shrouded the four wave diode rectifier and ignition coil. Failure to maintain the rear suspension plungers inevitably resulted in rear brake squeal.

work. I seem to remember Benny Marshall did a similar exercise on it as the one Reg and I did on the Indian Speed Twin. By this time, Anthony had obtained an English registration number for it, ULY 31.

I didn't know Anthony at this particular time; it wasn't until 1981 or '82, when I received a telephone call from him, that I recalled the little bike coming into the repair shop. He had married and by now had a 19-year-old son called Adam. Guess what? He wanted to do the trip again, this time with Adam on another Cub as company! Could I get ULY 31 ready for a return journey? he asked, and could I obtain another Cub for Adam, too? They wanted both bikes in top condition as they were going to ride them from their London home, down to the south coast, cross the Channel and then down to the Med and on to Alexandria. From there, they would ride straight down through the Sahara and all the way down to the bottom of Africa again, ending at Capetown.

What a daunting task, I thought, but I did it and they made it! Some of the things Anthony told me about his second trip made my hair stand on end, such as running the gauntlet of ragtag and bobtail African soldiers armed with the Russian Kalashnikov 'Widow Maker' automatic rifles; how they had to

The Great North Road in Southern Rhodesia, which certainly gave the suspension of ULY 31 a hammering!

*Anthony attending to the panniers
on ULY 31*

*Anthony Smith, son Adam and
ULY 31, before the bike was brought
to the author for restoration prior to
the second African journey.*

hide their watches and valuables to avoid having them confiscated as they crossed from border to border. Again, where angels fear to tread! Obviously, a book of this particularly courageous second journey was called for and is entitled *Smith and Son*.

Home again, and Adam went to Oxford to read medicine whilst Anthony did a super Radio 4 programme all about the journey. Being the sort of guy he is, though, he couldn't rest and promptly undertook a balloning trip over Africa, which he recounted in another book *Throw Out Two Hands*. The last I heard of him, Anthony was organising a steam-powered raft trip up the Congo, or was it the Orinoco? I expect he'll be in touch when he wants ULY 31 fettled to get it through the next MoT. Good luck, Anthony, my friend.

Back at Meriden, Mr Fields had retired, Albert Charlton had been made up from chargehand to foreman and Bert Carter had moved off the fitting bench to become chargehand. Good old Bert, ex-Royal Artillery sergeant and ex-desert rat, who fought off Italian soldiers of the Axis forces with nothing but a spade! He was a character; enormously good-looking with silver hair and always immaculately dressed. When Albert Charleton finally retired, Bert became foreman and Reg Hawkins chargehand, which

Would you believe that the author, pictured here, rebuilt a Cub from this in 1982, which writer, Anthony Smith, then rode from England to Cape Town?

was how it stayed right up to the end in 1973.

A regular visitor to the repair department was the SU carburettor man, Ginger Woods, an extraordinary character and one of the top class road racers in pre-war years, along with such folk as Harold Daniel and Freddie Frith. If we had a troublesome SU on a customer's Thunderbird, Ginger would come along and tune it, passing on to the repair shop chaps valuable tips into the bargain in the event the same problem arose in the future.

Originally, the Thunderbird - when introduced in 1949 - was equipped with the Amal-type 276 carburettor which had separate mixing and float chambers. Whether for reasons of economy or performance and quick response I don't know, the Amal was discontinued on the 6T in 1951 and for the 1952 season the 1.25 inch SU was introduced. The carb to air cleaner connection rubber on the Amal had to be quite severely cranked to miss the saddle down tube, which came to within an inch of the mixing chamber intake, on to which the rubber connector had to fit. Because the MC2 SU was slightly bulkier, clearance was even less with the result that it was impossible to fit the air cleaner connection rubber. A slight modification to the front frame was required and the rectangular air cleaner positioned behind the battery carrier had to be moved as well. By fitting a cast eye in the saddle down tube frame, the air cleaner connecting rubber could pass through the eye and fit straight on to the SU carb intake without any bends or kinks. We found that a connecting rubber with even the smallest kink in it would collapse under severe throttle openings due to the depression caused on what we called 'full suck.' (At a later date, we even fitted a steel sleeve inside the rubber connector to prevent this). As the connection was now straight, the air cleaner altered from rectangular to D-shaped and was positioned immediately behind the down tube, thus giving a straight flow from the cleaner through the eye in the frame to the carburettor intake. Not only did this improve performance on the SU-equipped 6T Thunderbird, it also gave superb economy.

One of the problems with the old slide-type Amals was that if the throttle was snapped open too quickly, the engine would not respond, very often cutting out. This was not the case with the SU, however. Even the normal production set SU carbs (those fitted on the track straight out of the box from SU) were a giant leap forward compared with the old Amal 276. You simply could not kill the motor by snapping open the throttle, so fast was the response. When Ginger tuned a troublesome instrument he would have the bike on its stand ticking over and then, placing the palms of his hands against the twistgrip, would roll the grip open so fast you would think he was spinning a top. The engines always responded and I never ever saw Ginger manage to stop a 6T Thunderbird by doing this. As he would point out to me, this was the beauty of the CV or constant vacuum carburettor as opposed to the conventional type. Whether it was cost or production problems, I don't know, but by 1958 the Thunderbird, now in its lovely Burnished Gold finish, was the last model to appear equipped with the SU carb; the 1959 Charcoal Grey 6T came equipped with the Amal Monobloc which had been the standard carb on all other twins since its introduction in 1955.

I last saw Ginger, with his little briefcase of beautiful SU tools, jets and so on, working on a 6T in 1956 just before my call-up. I never saw him again and, indeed, have not done so to this day, but I still remember him vividly tuning those superb SU carbs and the lessons I learned then have stood me in good stead during the course of my restorations.

Willie, the tomatoes - and black enamel ...

Les Williams was a rider and fitter in the Royal Signals Motorcycle Display Team during his national service and came to Meriden with the team to bring the bikes back for rework at the end of the riding display season. He applied for a job in the repair shop, secured it for when his army days were over and, after his demob, started his career at Meriden. As he originated from a small village in the Black Mountains of Brecon, called Cwm Du, lodgings obviously had to be found. Harold Dix, affectionately known as Dixie, took him in and Les was settled now, ready to start work. As his lodgings were on the same route home as my house, we used to ride home together; him on his TR5 and me on JRW 405. Sometimes on the way we had a bit of a do, with Les usually getting the better of me, due to superior riding skills gained whilst part of the White Helmets, as the Royal Corps of Signals Motorcycle Display Team was later called.

To appreciate Les (who became known as Willie), you had to understand his unusual sense of humour. He got up to all sorts of tricks, playing pranks on people in the repair shop mainly, although others outside weren't precluded. One of his favourite tricks was on the pipe smokers of the repair shop and Bert Marlow, Reg Hawkins and Ted Russell were the targets this time. Each had on the back of his workbench a Nescafe tin (before the glass jars with plastic screw lids came on the scene). The press-on lids had holes pierced in them and a few inches of white string pushed through, with about 3/16 of an inch poking out of the top. These tins were then filled, not quite to the top, with paraffin, which would capillary action up the wick (string). On arrival in the morning, once lit with a match they would burn all day with a small, clean flame from which these chaps could light their pipes again and again.

Willie would get to work in the morning five minutes early, empty the tins of paraffin and top them up with water, finally putting a few drops of paraffin in last (which floated on top of the water). The wick would soak up the paraffin and burn normally, but once this was all but gone the flame would splutter and finally die out. The amount of enjoyment he derived from watching each of the three blokes scratch their heads, wondering why their little lamps didn't stay alight! After all, when the lid was prised off, to all intents and purposes, it looked as if there was fuel still in there. Willie could keep this one going for days and the enjoyment was terrific, especially as old Bert Marlow and Ted used to live with their pipes in their mouths.

His other favourite trick, perpetrated on an unsuspecting Jimmy Davis, was to electrify the workbench and vice. Of course, Willie didn't want to hurt anyone seriously, just give them a little jolt. This was relatively easy to accomplish as all the workbenches had sheet steel tops with roll-over edges screwed down on to the thick wooden bench tops and thus insulated from earth. At the end of the bench, up at the top end of the workshop was the Mag-master machine, a superb piece of equipment driven by a single-phase electric motor with infinitely variable speed control from 1-7000rpm. In the fascia was a Smith's rev-counter by which it was possible to adjust the speed accurately. We would bolt on to this magnetos, ignition coils, distributors and alternators, connect them to sets of adjustable points, resistors and ammeters, and then set them running at a test speed. By varying the gaps on the adjustable points and making the magneto work harder, it was possible to see after a while whether the armature was starting to break down. There would be a nice, steady 'zzzzzzz' sound and a continuous purple/blue arc across the points on a good magneto at, say, 6000rpm. If it started to break down, the 'zzzzzz' sound would be intermittent and the spark a slightly lighter colour. A magneto could be left unattended, running quite happily for hours, so everyone was used to the noise.

No one saw Willie go up to the bench (he must have had a length of HT cable rolled up in his pocket) whilst this particular BTH magneto was running at something like 5000rpm. He waited for Jimmy to walk up to his vice, carrying a front frame and reaching for the vice handle with his free hand. Quick as a flash, Willie touched the end of his length of HT lead to the arcing terminal and dropped the other end on to the benchtop. Fortunately no other fitter, myself included, was working at his vice — just Jimmy. There was a howl, a 'clang' as the frame first of all went up in the air and then hit the floor, then a shout of rage as Jimmy came up the shop looking very wild-eyed. By this time, Willie and the HT lead had vanished ...

Willie was always joking about; it was his nature, so I decided to get him back - or so I thought ... When we got to work most mornings we would be wearing our Barbour suits and riding boots. We'd clock in and walk through the factory to the repair shop, where at our individual benches we'd take off our helmets and Second World War gas mask cases (everyone used these, slung over their shoulders as they made excellent lunch tin carriers). Next off would be the jacket to be hung up and, finally, by pushing down the over-trousers, you could step out of your riding boots and straight into your work shoes. One could now simply stand the boots and over-trousers under the bench, ready to jump into them at going-home time so as to effect a quick getaway.

My Dad was always a good gardener, and when his tomato plants bore fruit there were tomatoes for lunch every day: Mum would put cheese sandwiches and at least three tomatoes in my lunch box. I got fed up with tomatoes and, on this particular day, found an alternative use for a couple of them. I bided my time and, when Willie went to the toilet, pushed two over-ripe tomatoes into the toes of each of his riding boots! Trying my hardest to act normally during the working day and not think of what I'd done, I waited out what I felt was probably one of the longest, slowest days I'd ever lived. Come going-home time we went down to the toilets to wash our hands, where I lingered as long as I could so that Willie went into the workshop before me. Hardly able to contain myself, but as nonchalantly as possible, I proceeded to get my kit on whilst Willie, in his usual enthusiastic way, almost leapt into his riding boots. He'd got his over-trousers half-way up before he realised that something wasn't quite right deep down inside his boots. By this time I'd had to turn my back on him to prevent him from seeing my expression. As I looked around, pulling on my Barbour jacket at the same time to make my turn look as natural as possible, he was staring in utter disbelief at the soggy mess oozing from his socks and from between his toes. He must have seen my grin, because he said something very uncomplimentary in Welsh! With a grunt he put on his boots, got kitted up and followed me out to the bike sheds. Nothing more was said. We got on our bikes and set off home, me following him as usual. He was so quiet and that in itself should have warned me to stay on my guard.

A few days went by - nothing happened. Willie was his normal, irrepressible self, causing mayhem wherever he went, but nothing directed towards me: I couldn't believe this; no reprisals — not like him at all, I thought. Perhaps as I'm about to go into the army and take his place as the Display Team rider/fitter, he's decided not to damage me? No such luck! Going-home time saw the usual melee in and out of the washroom and accompanying good-natured banter like, "Bozzie [Joe Bosworth] you've got so many wrinkles across your forehead, when you screw your hat on, is it left or right-hand thread?" which elicited the succinct reply of "Bollocks!" from Joe.

I pulled on my riding boots and over-trousers very warily again for about the third time since the tomato incident — nothing — stranger and stranger. "Oh well," I thought, "Willie has let this one pass" but I should have known better. Fully kitted, with helmets on, we walked down to clock out and then on to the bike sheds. My Tiger started first prod as it always did. "That's a relief," I thought, "at least he's not messed about with JRW." Into gear, down the drive, out on to the A45, accelerate, into second, indicate left still in second and turn into Oak Lane. This was a twisty, cross-country route we always took to cut out the traffic on the A45 (then the main road between Birmingham and Coventry). The first 200 or 300 yards are fairly straight, then there's a tight left bend. The bike was in second gear, accelerating behind Willie on his TR5, when I reached up to pull down my MkVIII goggles atop my ACU pudding basin helmet and, suddenly, everything went black! I couldn't see a bloody thing and rode straight into the ditch although, luckily, by the time I took the dive I wasn't going too quickly. Willie must have been wetting himself! He never even came back; he was probably pretty sure that everything was okay. When I picked myself and the bike up, I looked at my MkVIII goggle lenses: the rotten sod had painted them with black enamel!

Goodbye ...

That wasn't the only time I fell off my bike going home as, a few days before I was to leave for Catterick Garrison to report for my national service, I came an almighty cropper! It was pure sloppiness in my riding that caused it as, by then, I reckoned I was the bee's knees on my Tiger: even now, after all these years, it sets my teeth on edge to think of the things I did. Anyway, on this particular Wednesday night I wanted to get home early as I had a date with Gloria. I even out-distanced Willie, speeding down Oak Lane, round the left and right, accelerating hard along the straight, then diving slightly right down the Woodyard hill to the medium right bend at the bottom, by which time, I suppose, I was doing 50 to 55mph. Cranking over for the right-hander — horror of horrors — the back end started to slide out. Unable to control it, I had to let JRW go; as I bounced along I saw her hit a telegraph pole smack amidships about two feet off the ground. Lying there stunned and dazed, I was aware of a pain in my right foot on the inside of the ankle and, upon looking down, I could see that my right boot had been torn off, my sock was in shreds with blood oozing out of a hole just below my ankle bone.

That didn't worry me so much, as I was pretty numb at that moment and couldn't feel a lot, but my beloved JRW was ruined. Even lying there I could see the frame was bent, as were the forks. The exhaust system was a mess and one of the Burgess silencers had been smashed through the rear spring-hub. Oh God! I was leaving in two days and needed my bike to travel on - what was I going to do? All these thoughts flashed through my mind as I lay there and others who used the lane began to arrive - Willie, Reg Hawkins and the Wainfleet coach carrying Triumph workers to various drop-offs on the way to Nuneaton (for people who had no personal transport and didn't live on a regular bus route. For a fixed weekly fee they could be picked up and dropped off outside their homes or at the end of their streets and ride to work in comfort, reading the morning paper).

Just along the lane was the local police house, occupied by Bill Streathers and his wife. I was given a lift there and Bill efficiently dressed my damaged ankle whilst his darling wife made me a hot, sweet cup of tea. Unbeknown to me Reg Hawkins, dear old Reg, had hightailed it back to the factory on his combo and got the works box combo out. With the aid of another he got JRW into the box and took her back to the repair shop.

After a while, Reg called at the police house, telling me "Don't worry about your bike, I've taken it back to the workshop so at least it'll be safe." Thanking Sergeant Streathers and his wife, I rather stiffly boarded GKP 15 and Reg took me home at a leisurely pace. As I was somewhat later than usual, my Mum was standing at the end of the entry to our house when we pulled up. She nearly threw a fit when I tried to tell her what had happened, but luckily Reg said something like "It was wet tar, Mrs Hancox — he didn't stand a chance." That seemed to smooth things over somewhat and Reg said "I shouldn't come in tomorrow; rest up and I'll collect you on Friday at about twenty to eight. I'll also tell them at the factory, but they'll know by tomorrow morning anyway, as the story will have got back by then." With that I bade him farewell, my Mum thanked him and I sat there, awaiting my Dad's arrival home from work and his comments on my unfortunate escapade. My first thoughts were "Glo will be waiting. What will my Dad say?" I need not have worried as he was pretty good about it and even walked up to the local telephone box and rang Gloria (we didn't have a 'phone, but as her parents were in business, they did). About an hour later, she came in, looking all worried and flustered. Mum and Dad went out that night and left us to ourselves: I couldn't move much but, still, it was one of the best nights I can ever remember!

Friday morning came all too soon and Reg arrived on good old GKP 15 to collect me, as he said he would. I felt rather strange that morning, not from the bumps, grazes and stiffness, but because I knew that this was the last time for two years I'd be going to Meriden. Whilst I was still upstairs, Reg took out to his combo my riding coat and helmet (I didn't know this until later in the day). We set off for the works - about a twenty minute run from my house in Coventry - arriving in time to hobble to the clocking-in machine. It was dead on 8am, Friday 18 May 1956.

As Reg and I walked slowly into the repair shop, a huge cheer and cacophony of banging spanners on steel worktops started. I've never experienced mickey-taking like it, either before or since! If you fall off when you work in a motorcycle factory I guess you must expect something like this. I must have looked amazed, because Mr Fields came up to me and said "Well young man, it's your last day. Get on with something." Reg, Joe, Benny and everyone was smiling which I attributed to the fact that this "cocky young bugger" had come a cropper and was now paying penalty points in the shape of a good ribbing!

Before I did anything, I had to look at JRW to see if I could repair it ready for the following week. I knew that I was going to need it for travelling but the last time I had seen it, bouncing off a telegraph pole, it didn't look as if it was going anywhere. I asked Mr Fields where my bike was. "It's down at the bottom of the shop on the last bench" he said. I hobbled down the length of the workshop , speaking to the blokes and answering their questions as quickly as I could. At last I saw JRW 405, but it wasn't my bike, as there were no numbers on it. I couldn't believe it — she was brand new: not only had the frame been changed, there were new forks, petrol tank, mudguards, new springwheel and, what I didn't know at the time of the accident, was that the impact

A close-up in 1992 of the telegraph pole, which still bears the scars from 1957 ...

against the pole, especially on the exhaust pipes, had ripped the screw-in adaptors out of the close-pitched fin alloy head, but now she had a new head as well.

Just then old Ted from the paint shop appeared with my front and rear number plates, freshly sign-written: JRW 405. To say I was speechless is an understatement; I didn't know whether to laugh or cry as everyone just stood around smiling at me. I couldn't speak and was afraid that if I tried I'd start blubbering. Mr Fields saved the day by coming up to me and putting a hand on my shoulder, saying "Look on this as a going away present." I was finally overwhelmed and escaped to the toilets and cried.

Basic training

Dad came with me on JRW 405 to Coventry station on the morning of my departure and, after saying cheerio to each other, he rode off on the Tiger. It sounded gorgeous. Showing my warrant I went through on to platform 2 to await the arrival of the train to Derby, where I would change for Leeds, finally getting to Richmond in Yorkshire at about 11pm. As I looked around the platform I noticed quite a few young chaps, all with that scared look in their eyes. I thought "Surely I don't look like that?" but I did ...

One of them approached me and said just one word "Catterick?" I nodded. His name was Fred Sutton and we palled up for mutual moral support, I guess, and stuck together all the way to Richmond. We got there about 10 minutes past 11, it was pitch black and obviously we were a bit timid, to say the least, as we got off the train. Somehow even the air smelt different. It was so quiet as well, with no traffic noise. Then came an almighty bellow from down the platform "All you lot for Vimy Lines, fall in outside on the double!" It was a voice straight from hell which emanated from a bullet-headed sergeant with a mouth as big as Grangemouth. We all stumbled outside, where four Bedford three-tonner lorries were waiting with engines ticking over. It was a short ride to the section of Catterick camp called Vimy Lines, where we were ordered to get out and form three ranks, and from there marched to the cookhouse, where we were informed by the sergeant, at the top of his voice, that we should get something to eat and drink before being put to bed.

Bustling into the cookhouse, we were met with the smell of sizzling bacon. '"Great!" I thought. First of all, we had a mug of horrible-tasting tea slapped down in front of us (which I later discovered contained bromide to prevent us getting thoughts about home and girlfriends). The sizzling bacon was for the sergeant and we got a thick slice of bread spread with margarine and a quarter-inch thick layer of red jam. I was hardly able to drink the tea because of its funny taste, and after only about two mouthfuls of bread and jam, the sergeant started yelling at us again. Off we trooped to our barrack room where we all got into bed and lay, trying our hardest to drop off to sleep. With so much going through my mind, it was almost impossible and as I lay there thinking "God, two years, two bloody years" I heard several of the chaps start to sob very softly in their beds. It took all I had not to start as well, but I thought "Well, you're here; make the best of it" and eventually fell into an exhausted, fitful sleep.

The next morning we were awakened at six and, after completing our ablutions, were marched over to the cookhouse for breakfast. Another mug of that horrible-tasting tea, a couple of rashers of barely-cooked, fatty bacon and a piece of the queerest egg I have ever seen which came from a 2 inch deep, 3 foot square steel tray which was blackened with burnt grease. The cook simply cracked sufficient eggs to fill the tin tray and put them on the stove. If he did this at 6.30 to 7am, by the time the cookhouse was opened for breakfast the fried eggs had taken on the consistency of leather! With a sharp knife, he cut this mess into approximately 4x5 inch pieces and each person had one of these slopped on to his plate - it was enough to turn your stomach.

Afterward breakfast we were marched over to the QM stores and issued with our kit. Getting back to the barrack room, we got into our new, hairy uniforms and, with the square of brown paper and length of string we had each been given, wrapped up our civilian clothes, finally writing on the parcel our respective home addresses. This last act was our final severance with anything to do with civilian life or home and it really underlined the fact that we were in the army now!

Next came the dreaded jabs. We were marched over to the medical centre, lined up with tunics off and shirt sleeves rolled up as high as we could get them and, in turn, received three injections in one arm and two in the other. I was okay, but several chaps went down before it came to their turns; big, tough Teddy boys from London and hard men from Glasgow fainted as well! Later on, in the barrack room we all laughed about it: somehow we were already getting an all-for-one and one-for-all feeling.

The following ten weeks - basic training - were pure hell. I was with a good bunch of blokes, but all of them, like me, had never left the comfort of their homes before, where Mum always did the cleaning up, cooked the meals and generally looked after you. This was another world! The two full corporals and one lance-corporal were the instructors who instilled fear into us: fear of being the last out of the washroom in the morning; fear of not having your kit ready for inspection and, most of all, fear of relegation. This word haunted you as you knew that if you failed on anything you might be relegated back to the intake coming in after yours, which meant doing it all over again. This is what drove me on.

Some chaps went into the Army with the attitude "Bugger the Army, I'll do just what I have to and no more" but they soon changed their tune. Over the ensuing weeks the corporals slowly but surely broke us, made us cry, spat at us, kicked us, took us on drill parades until we dropped, woke us up at 3 o'clock in the morning to get on with cleaning our kit, only to make us crawl through mud the following day when we were wearing the same stuff. I never did understand the object of the exercise then. I was only 19 and not into psychology, but it worked: before we knew it we weren't individuals as we had been when we came in, but a team. Suddenly, the interesting stuff started and not just drill, marching, barking orders (each chap took turns at taking the troop). We now got to handle the Lee-Enfield .303 No 4, the Bren Mk2 and the 9mm parabellum Sten gun and, if we were good boys, Corporals Garnham and Ellis told us, we'll show you the hand grenades as well! We were all issued with our own Lee-Enfield rifle and suddenly everyone in the troop was as keen as mustard. We were taught about the working parts by little Lance-Corporal Maurice Ankrum by way of an enjoyable guessing game, one half of the troop against the other, trying to catch each other out.

Suddenly there was a togetherness when we marched. We were nearing the end of our initial training period and, if you did well on range classification, there was only the final passing-out parade of the whole regiment, wearing best uniform and in front of the Colonel-in-Chief. There was usually a competition throughout the ten weeks, with each troop in the regiment being awarded points for the individual training and assessment periods. Our troop was running fairly close with 10 Troop, and it all hinged on the Regimental Sergeant Major who would eye very critically our drill and marching during the parade, deciding, afterwards, which was the best troop.

For the range classification we were marched up to the 30 yard range at the back of Vimy Lines. There we were to fire the Sten and Webley revolver at man-sized targets. Basically, the Sten was a makeshift weapon for house-to-house fighting, brought into being during the war and chambered to use captured enemy (German) 9mm rounds (most of the German hand guns and machine pistols were 9mm). It was an awful thing to fire and I could never manage to hit the man-sized target, never mind place the shots on repetition (single shot, one every time you squeezed the trigger). On auto (bursts of fire for as long as you held the trigger) or later on as we called it full auto or 'rock and roll,' it was uncomfortable. Corporal 'Scouse' Ellis was a wizard with the Sten and could make an empty Andrews Liver Salt can jump repeatedly on single shots. I'm afraid I wasn't much better with the Webley, but at least I could hit the target. They still shouted at us things like "Bloody hell, son, you frightened him then!" or "Hit it, hit it, you dozy man; nobody ever died of a near miss!"

The hand grenade or Mills bomb was something that always struck terror into me. Yet, handled correctly, they were no trouble at all, said our instructor. Ha ha! Up on the range, there was an old farmhouse which was used for hand grenade practice. We were first taught the textbook stance of left foot forward, left arm outstretched and a right over-arm throw. "I suppose that's okay, if there's no sod shooting at you" I thought. The next thing was to place one on the run, through one of the windows. Everything went fine, until the chap in front of me took his turn. He was nervous, and it didn't make him feel any better when our intrepid Corporal Ellis said "These things are live, and they can kill you." He started his run, pulled the pin out and, as he passed the window, lobbed it in with his right arm. It looked good, but suddenly he stopped, turned round and walked back. We couldn't believe it, the grenade had struck part of the window frame and bounced out and he had gone back to pick it up and chuck it again. Needless to say, he only just made it. Corporal Ellis was purple — he couldn't speak for a few seconds — then he came out with words I'd never heard before! It really was nearly a tragedy, although at the same time there was a funny side to it.

Our next outing was to the range. I've never been sure since my army days just where the range was situated. Most of the Yorkshire Moors where we practised, especially on the bikes, was MoD land which is now the Yorkshire Moors National Park, but I think it was at a place called Strenshall, just off the

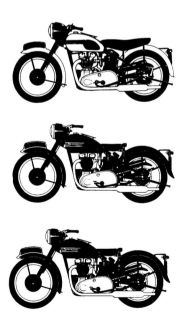

road to York. The range was 1000, 800 and 600 yards. It was a splendid day, with bright sunshine and only a light breeze. There were no sounds except the baa-ing of sheep and the odd curlew calling, and that was it, we were in the wilderness. There was a field telephone from the firing line down to the butts and only white markers visible for the different distances. We unloaded from the two three-ton Bedford trucks: 13 troop, two corporals, one lance-corporal and a captain whom I'd never seen before.

We all lined up with our own rifles and were issued with four clips of five rounds each of .303 inch full metal jacket ammunition. By now I was so eager I was nearly bursting. I'd always been a good shot (only with air guns, mind) and I thought "Could do yourself a bit of good here." We'd all sat in the barrack room at night, with the clip and five dummy rounds, practising the loading technique and flipping out the empty clip when all five had been smoothly and quickly pressed down through the open breech and into the short magazine. We were going to shoot two clips of five from the kneeling position and then the remaining two clips from the prone position. The captain had got into one of the three-tonners and gone off up to the butts to check on his men and the targets when Corporal Ellis shouted for us to gather round. He said "Look lads, as a bit of an incentive, chip in a shilling apiece. Winner takes all." As our weekly pay was just £1 and £1 10s 0d (£1.50) alternately, most of which was going on food in the NAAFI at night or stamps and writing paper (I was writing a letter a day to Gloria), we faltered a bit, but then thought "Someone must win" and chipped in a bob apiece which amounted to quite a tidy sum of money.

The Bedford came back and everything was ready. The Captain rang the butts, the butts rang the Captain. "First ten men!" yelled Scouse Ellis. I was well back, so had an opportunity to watch and learn. He gave the command to load "Safety catches on, aim, safety catches off, fire in your own time. Carry on." I didn't expect the noise to be so loud or sharp; I'd never been close to a .303 going off before. I thought "Sugar, this is going to hurt my shoulder." I didn't do so well in the kneeling position, but when prone got six out of ten bulls, the other four were magpies, or something, I can never remember — only the six bulls! It hadn't been done before on a basic training intake; squaddies had even closed their eyes just before loosing one off and gone completely off the board! Suddenly the corporals were patting me on the back and saying "Where did you learn to shoot like that?"and, in the heat of the moment I lied, saying as nonchalantly as possible "Oh, I shoot for the West Midlands Gas Rifle Team." (I didn't, of course, but my Dad had once upon a time). The lot of us then loaded up into the three-tonners after standing in ranks, holding the rifle at the port, rattling the bolt backwards and forwards three or four times, and speaking the words "Sir, I have no live rounds or empty cases in my possession, Sir" to the Captain as he stood in front of each of us in turn.

We were all elated when we got back to barracks, me more than anyone, but then came the blow. Another chap had done well in the kneeling position and quite well in the prone. When his two scores were added, they equalled mine. We shared the money and both of us took the whole troop to the NAAFI and blew the lot in one go. I suppose that's what mates are for, isn't it?

Our troop, at passing out parade time, was equal with 10 Troop, so it was all down to drill and marching, watched by the RSM's eagle eye. Corporals Ellis and Garnham and Lance Corporal Ankrum were now totally different people to the ones who had been putting us through all the torments of hell for the past ten weeks. Suddenly, they came into the barrack room smiling, just like normal people and no longer the men who, a couple of weeks ago, would stick their face close to yours, yelling and spitting, while you were rigidly standing to attention, looking at a point just above the horizon. They shouted, cajoled, paced around you, bawled in your ear and ridiculed you in front of everybody. Now it was all over and you just had to do your best for them on the parade. It would show they were good instructors, wouldn't it, if you won the "stick," an ornate silver-knobbed cane which was presented to the Instructor if his troop won.

We were perfect and Scouse Ellis won the stick. We were all pleased.

Ripon

Standing on the parade square with my kit, I awaited the arrival of the transport that was going to take me to Ripon and Harper Barracks. Out of all the regiment, I was the only one posted to Ripon as a despatch rider; no-one else made it which I often, in later years, thought extremely odd.

The other lines of men were loading into Bedford QLs, three-tonners and such like, but I stood there all on my lonesome thinking "What the Hell have I got myself into?" After about three quarters of an hour, a Land-Rover screamed across the parade ground and screeched to a halt in front of me. A chap with a battered, lived-in face beneath an oily beret leaned over to the passenger door and shouted "Hancox, Ripon. Get in." I hurriedly threw my kit bag and hold-all into the Land-Rover, jumping into the passenger seat beside the driver, who I noticed was a full Corporal. We shot off the parade ground with me sitting to attention, not daring to breath until spoken to. The Corporal had his beret shoved to the back of his head, a tunic that was definitely not in its prime and no belt on. I thought, "Hell, who is this man, driving like Mike Hawthorn. We'll never get to Ripon alive!"

We roared out of Catterick, along the concrete rafted tank road, towards Scotton, Newton-le-Willows, Masham and Grewelthorpe. The driver - William Gunn but known as Ben - was, in thirty years time, to become my comforter in some of the worst hours of my life. Ben was later my driving instructor and also doubled as the squadron driver when no-one else was available. Later still, Ben - a true friend - would come to my aid on the death of another good friend at Ripon.

At Harper Barracks, Ripon, was based the Royal Signals Motor Cycle Display Team. I had only to complete my trade training as a despatch rider and I could be posted into "The Team," as it was called. Trade training was a series of sequences intended to turn an ordinary, non-motorcycling person into a competent DR (despatch rider). I was riding a 100mph Tiger back and forwards each weekend with a colleague on pillion but had to forget all that and

The author standing (rather self-consciously!) outside 92 'spider' at Harper Barracks, Ripon in 1957.

learn to ride the Army way! It really was a joke to us. Several chaps had BSA Gold Stars, one had an International Norton. Several others had various makes of twin cylinder 500s or 650s, and yet we had to learn all over again how to master the side-valve single M20! If we got too cocky and started acting the fool, our instructor, Corporal Taffy McTiffin, would make us get off the bike, stop the motor and push it for miles. He wasn't a motorcyclist in Civvy Street; you could tell that by the way he rode — elbows wide and up in the air! Someone remarked as he rode down the camp road one day "There he goes, he looks just like Glenn Ford riding a bloody horse!" I didn't twig what he meant then, but years later, when watching an old Western starring Glenn Ford on TV, I realized. Yes, he really did look like Glenn Ford riding a horse!

The trade training went along normally, taking in all aspects of Army motorcycling, such as maintenance, fiddling the speedos and fiddling the petrol (well, how else could you manage to get home each weekend on your own bike?). We were still only getting £1 10s 0d and £1 alternate weeks, which mostly still went on food or, for smokers, fags.

Payday was on a Thursday at 11.00 hours in a designated barrack room with Lieutenant Payne, the pay officer, in charge. You had to queue outside with your paybooks and, when your turn, march smartly up to the front of the trestle table, behind which he was sitting. Coming to a smart halt, you saluted, picked up your money and shouted "Pay and paybook correct, Sir," you would then salute once more, about turn and march out. During my two year stint I went through this ritual around 101 times and I don't think the pay officer ever lifted his head to look at me once!

During trade training someone must have thought I was a likely lad because I got made up to Lance Corporal and put in charge of the section, which comprised all the chaps that were housed in the wing of the barracks, I suppose about eighteen or twenty in all. Ripon was a garrison town from the First World War and Harper Barracks - where we were - and Deverill Barracks on the other side of the road, were built to house troops before they were sent to the Western Front. Deverill Barracks now belonged to the Royal Engineers and Harper Barracks to the Royal Corps of Signals. All the barracks were built of wood and commonly called 'spiders', mainly, I suppose, because their plan-view was in the form of a central section which housed the ablutions — wash-room, toilets and drying room.

When looking around at the men of the section, one of the things that did strike home was that the Army took no account generally of your civilian occupation. Knowing most of the chaps and what they did in Civvy Street, it really surprised me that they all ended up in this particular barrack room to learn how to become despatch riders. I found that bakers or chefs ended up in the Motor Transport Section as mechanics. Conversely, mechanics in Civvy Street found themselves behind a teleprinter, and electricians, instead of becoming driver-electricians, became despatch riders.

I was very lucky, I suppose, to get to Ripon as a despatch rider, especially as there were other motorcyclists in my troop at Catterick, one of whom actually worked for AMC Motorcycles at Plumstead in London. Amongst the section, however, was a person, whose name was Youall, who just did not have it in him to be on or anywhere near a motorcycle. Even after concerted attention and tuition, he could no more coordinate his hand and feet movements than fly, and simply to get him to engage first gear and move off was a feat in itself, whilst changing gear on the move was a wonder to behold.

Tales of Triumph & Meriden

The BSA war department M20 500cc side-valve, single cylinder motorcycle was built like a tank, and I'm convinced that Youall would have killed any other make of bike stone-dead, such was his inability to ride. After about three weeks he was able to start up the machine, engage first gear and ride away, changing up through the gears until he was finally in top. Under the watchful eye of the other Corporal and myself, he gave quite a passable performance.

On a particularly fine day in July, Nobby Clarke, the other Corporal, and I, each on a G3L Matchless WD motorcycle, took our motley crew of eighteen, M20-mounted trainees, dressed in their DR coats and boots, tin crash-helmets and yellow gauntlets, out along the road from Ripon towards Sutton under Whitestone Cliffe, a small village on the Pickering to Scarborough Road and under the shadow of the Hambledon Hills. The village is at the foot of one of the steepest zigzag climbs in the Yorkshire Dales, with the road twisting and turning until it finally emerges on top of Sutton Bank. This is probably the finest view of the Dales in all Yorkshire which is nowadays a popular tourist spot. Even many years later, on better road surfaces and in a modern motor car, one has to be very careful not to fluff a gear change, especially on the very acute hairpin bends, where forward speed drops to almost a walking pace. On a motorcycle, if you were adept, there was no problem . Even the M20s, ridden at walking pace in either second or bottom gear, would pull up the side of a house.

With Nobby heading the little convoy, we attacked the first part of the hill at a spanking forty miles per hour. I was looking after the rearmost riders in the little convoy, ensuring there were no problems. After rounding the first bend, I noticed that some of the trainees were moving out and passing a rider who seemed to be slowing down more and more. Hanging back, and now at the third leg of the climb, I saw to my horror that it was Youall, hunched over the handlebars, staring fixedly ahead. As I rode up by his side, he had a funny look on his face and I could tell instantly that he wasn't enjoying himself one bit. I could also tell that the poor old M20 was still in top gear and slogging so hard as to almost stall, as I yelled to him "Youall, change down, change down!" We were fast coming up to another acute bend and I knew that any minute the motor on his bike would give up, having to pull too high a gear at too low a road speed. In desperation, I rode closer to him on his off-side and, reaching out with my left foot, kicked his gearlever upwards. It was a spur-of-the-moment action on my part but it worked. With a horrible shudder, his engine started to rev more freely and we proceeded up the climb towards the final bend. Quite pleased with myself, I shouted "keep going, keep going," whereupon Youall did one of those meaningless things that you do when panic has your heart in its icy grip: with slow deliberation he reached out with his left hand and pulled in the clutch lever. I slammed on my brakes and sat watching in amazement as, with motor racing fit to bounce the valves, the M20 - deprived of drive - quickly slowed to a stop and started to roll backwards down the steep incline. As Youall passed me he had both feet down on the road to keep himself upright, the engine was still racing away and he stared fixedly ahead, hands on the handlebars as if welded there.

By now, Nobby had stopped the little convoy on level ground at the top of the hill and come back to see what was going on. He rode straight past me, shouting to Youall "Put the brakes on!" but to no avail. By the time I turned around and started down the steep hill after them, Nobby was stationary on the hairpin bend silently staring at the three broken fence railings through which Youall and the M20 had disappeared into the undergrowth. Leaving our bikes on their side-stands, we clambered through the ferns and black-berry brambles until we found him and the bike, both surprisingly undam-aged. Nobby hauled Youall to his feet, told him to get on behind me and, whilst I rode to the waiting members of the section with him, Nobby followed on the M20. Making the nervous trainee despatch rider sit on his bike, I took Nobby down to collect his G31 Matchless which was still by the broken fence. All the way to Whitby we watched Youall very closely, but even on the home-ward journey and coming down Sutton Bank he rode well and gave us no further cause for alarm.

In the NAAFI that night we recounted the day's escapade to the other Instructors and, after much debating, came to the conclusion that, faced with such a daunting climb, he panicked and his mind blanked out what little he knew. We all agreed that he'd never make a motorcyclist.

That wasn't the only trainee trouble that occurred whilst I was taking part in the three months' trade training period. During a training ride we came back via Catterick camp and along the back road to Ripon. This entailed pro-ceeding out of the garrison town of Catterick and along the concrete surfaced tank road towards Thornton-Watlass crossroads, heading towards Masham. There was no kerb or ditch on either side at this point; the road simply stopped and the moorland scrub and heather began. Therefore, if you wished to stop, you just pulled over, off the concrete and on to the moorland which came right up to the roadside.

The engineers had been out along the tank road earlier on in the week, dropping off freshly-creosoted telephone poles at regular intervals alongside the road, a few feet into the heather. I seem to remember there was a pole about every thirty or forty yards, laying with its thick end in the direction of oncoming traffic. I was riding in my customary tail-end Charlie position as the little convoy of M20-mounted trainees, with Nobby out at the front, proceeded along the tank road. We must have been doing about forty miles an hour when I noticed that one of the trainees was starting to wander from side to side, getting ever nearer the edge of the concrete road surface. I thought to myself "The silly bugger has fallen asleep" and before I could accelerate and ride up by his side, he drifted off the concrete altogether.

What happened next will be imprinted in my memory for evermore. The M20 suddenly stopped dead, almost as if had run into an invisible brick wall, and the luckless trainee was catapulted some twenty to twenty-five feet out in front of his upright but motionless machine. In what seemed like slow motion he flew through the air, arms outstretched, his hands frantically grabbing for the controls. His must have been the rudest of awakenings, for it was clear he really didn't know where the hell he was. I watched in awe as, with his DR coat billowing, he sailed through the air like some grotesque leaping frog and landed, spread-eagled, face down in the heather.

Nobby, during one of his quick look-backs had noticed that I'd pulled up and, stopping the convoy, raced back to me to find out what the problem was. We both put our bikes on their prop-stands and ran over to the trainee, who was by now sitting up with a dazed "Where-am-I?" look on his face. Making a supreme effort not to laugh, Nobby asked him to get up and make sure that everything still worked. As the poor chap struggled to his feet and looked down at his muddy boots, the metal outer shell of his War Department tin crash helmet, which had somehow become partially detached from the lining during the flight, came off his head and flopped over, hanging upside down from his left ear. The stitching on one side of his helmet which held the leather and webbing chin-harness to the main part, had broken and allowed the steel outer case to hang there like an upturned basin. As gently as he could, Nobby lifted the lid upwards and over and, patting it firmly in place said, "Come on, lad, let's have a look at your bike."

We walked back the nine or ten paces to where the M20 stood, silent and still. It was only when we realised that we were walking alongside one of the poles that it dawned on us what had happened. The front wheel of the M20 had narrowly missed the end of the pole and passed to the left-hand side of it, with the timing side crankcase and timing cases taking full impact: the force was so great that it broke both the engine crankcase and timing cases, embedding pieces of broken aluminium in the end grain of the telephone pole. There was quite a big hole in the front of the poor old M20's motor, and amongst the oil and debris you could actually see the flywheel, but it hadn't moved the pole an inch! I stayed behind with the section whilst Nobby rode back to camp at Ripon and came back in a one-tonner. We lifted the M20 and its rider into the back and with myself leading the convoy and Nobby bringing up the rear, we made our weary way back to camp.

Good friendships were forged in the army, lasting friendships that only death can put an end to. One such friendship was with Nobby who originated from Hampton-in-Arden, near Meriden. We hit it off immediately and before long were going home together at the weekends on my Tiger 100, he to his Sylvia and me to Gloria.

For some unknown reason, religious instruction from the camp Padre was always on Saturday mornings in the cinema. Nobby and I marched our sections up to this every Saturday, then sneaked off out the back way to get ready for going home on the bike. You could, without seeking permission and provided you were not on any duties, leave camp at 12 noon on a Saturday, but had to be back in time for first parade at 8 o'clock on Monday morning, otherwise you were absent without leave and liable for a stretch in the guardroom.

As most of our wages had already been spent on food, it became an absolute must to obtain fuel from somewhere, otherwise we just wouldn't have enough to get home. At this time there was petrol rationing due to the Suez crisis, so, without coupons, you didn't stand an earthly of getting juice. But as Nobby and I were courting strong, we just had to get home each weekend, which is where the fiddle came in.

There was a Corporal, who shall be nameless but whom I've known since my army days and still come into contact with through motorcycling, who was a dab hand at manipulating speedos. Nowadays, second-hand car merchants 'clock' cars to remove mileage but we'd put it on! Knowing roughly how many miles a BSA M20, Matchless G3L or a Bedford three-ton truck did to the gallon helped, but all you did was take the speedo head to this Corporal, tell him how much fuel you required and he'd put on the appropriate miles to cover it. You simply filled in your works ticket accordingly to make things tally. Easy! By Friday, Nobby and I usually had a fire-bucket full of juice under the bed ready to put into JRW 405. As the bike was kept at the back of the Garrison Theatre it was easy during a normal day to walk down through the camp with a fire-bucket full of what appeared to be water from a distance. We had a Tundish (funnel) hidden by the bike, so it was quick and easy to fill her up in one go! When I think now of at the things we did I shiver because, if we had been caught, it would have been Colchester Military Prison for sure. Anyway, we did it and got away with it.

For 35 years Nobby and I have talked about what we did then, who we knew and asking do you remember old so-and-so questions? Three years ago, during a meal at one of our local hostelries, Nobby, his wife Sylvia, Gloria and I were talking old times when Nobby said how much he'd like to see the old place again. The girls said "Well, why don't you two clear off for the day and go?" so we arranged to go on Saturday 18 February 1988; a fateful day. Spot on time, Nobby pulled up outside my house and, saying cheerio to Gloria, we set off in my car; it was 7.30am exactly. We pulled into the town square at Ripon at 9.50am, enjoying a good run on a bright, sunny day with only light traffic on the M1. We first of all stood outside the bank building where, as Corporals, we would often be seconded to act as guard to Lt Payne and his driver when they had to collect the camp wages. This meant that you rode your Matchless G3L (all instructors and corporals had G3L machines; squaddies had M20s) behind the Land-Rover to the bank, pulled up behind, put the bike on its side-stand and ran round to open the door for the Lieutenant. Oh yes —

The author on his Matchless G3L during a practice session at Ripon.

you had drawn from the armoury a Sten gun and empty magazine which was slung across your chest. While the officer went into the bank, his driver kept the Land-Rover running and you had to stand outside with the Sten cocked and looking mean. The officer would come out, you'd 'cover' him to the Land-Rover and wait until he was in and it was moving off before de-cocking the Sten and leaping on to the Matchless to give chase. What a charade! I don't know what we were supposed to do if anyone tried anything — maybe club 'em to death with an empty gun!

All these things went through our minds as Nobby and I wandered around, looking and remembering. We already knew that Ben Gunn had elected to stay in Ripon upon his de-mob, because he'd married a local girl. We found that the old pub, where we often went for a drink, was still in business although it no longer went under the name of The Black Dog. Nobby said "I wonder what the camp is like now?" so into the car we leapt and drove the mile or so up Clotherholme Road to our old barracks. It had changed; all the old wooden spiders had gone, as had the wooden guardroom and squadron offices with their verandas. They were replaced with purpose-built brick buildings. The layout of the place looked the same, though, and we could still see the parade square - that hallowed ground — where no soldier dared tread in case the Sergeant Major saw you.

As soon as we pulled up outside the camp gates a soldier in full battle kit

The bank in Ripon town square has changed little since the author rode shotgun for the camp pay officer in 1958.

with the new SS80 Enfield marched up to us and asked us what we were doing. Nobby looked at him and said "Look, son, we were here before you were born." Nobby, ever the opportunist asked "I don't suppose there's any chance of looking around the old dump, is there?" We were told to bring the car in and park it opposite the guard room. I was conscious all the while of being watched closely, not only by our young friend with the SS80 (and I bet that it was loaded) but also by people behind the darkened glass of the guard-room windows from where a Sergeant emerged and asked us for some form of identification. Nobby had nothing on him but I had my driving licence which satisfied the Sergeant. We were given a soldier as an escort and off we went.

My, how it had all changed, so different to what we remembered. We did find all the petrol points and the FAMTO stores were still the same, but the NAAFI had gone, as had the cookhouse along with all the spiders. Never mind, it was worth going, just to walk the roads around the camp again and drink in the memories. Nobby was quite excited, pointing and actually laughing out loud at what used to go on where, and the things we got up to. Soon we were back at the guard room, shaking hands with everyone in sight, giving our thanks, and then with cheery waves we set off back to town.

We parked in the car park behind the Unicorn Hotel and sat in the lounge there, looking out of the big bay windows at the bustling square whilst we had coffee. We decided to see if old Ben Gunn was drinking in what we knew as The Black Dog (Ben was the driver who came to Catterick on passing-out parade day to take me, as the only DR posting, to Ripon in his Land-Rover). Nobby and I left the car where it was and started to walk to The Black Dog, not too far away. Once there, we asked if Ben came in on Saturdays and were told by the landlord that if he'd done the shopping he'd be in the Wheatsheaf by now. This pub was on the Harrogate road, about three-quarters of a mile away, but still within the confines of the built-up area, and in Ripon. Rather than walk back for the car, we elected to stroll there; after all it was a beautiful day and the sun was shining. We talked excitedly about Ben or, as Nobby put it, "Ben the old bugger" and wondered what his crinkly face would do when he saw us.

We arrived at 12.45pm exactly and stood in the crowded bar until I could catch the barmaid's eye to order. Both Nobby and I fancied light ales, so whilst she was opening the bottles and putting the glasses on the bar I asked her if Ben Gunn came in. "He'll be here anytime now" she replied, just as I turned to hand Nobby his bottle of beer and glass. As I reached forward to pick up my own bottle and glass, Nobby gave out a small cry and fell against me, knocking over both myself and a table next to me. God, I didn't know what was happening. I knelt on the bar-room floor, cradled his head and within seconds he was gone. Pandemonium broke out in the bar, but everyone was very good and the ambulance arrived within minutes. I just knelt there stunned as they put an oxygen mask on him and tried to revive him, but to no avail. They took us both to Harrogate Hospital in the ambulance, where I was taken to a small quiet room to be interviewed, first by a friendly nurse who took Nobby's particulars, address, next of kin, age and so on, and then by a very understanding policeman (about the same age as myself, I think). He wanted to link up by 'phone to Nobby's house in Coventry and for me to break the news to Sylvia, at the same instant having a policewoman call at the house in case Sylvia needed help.

It was the most awful phone call I've ever had to make. Afterwards, I signed for Nobby's belongings and took them back with me to Ripon. It had been a hell of a day. The police wouldn't let me drive home that evening as I was in shock and Maureen and David Small, owners of the Unicorn Hotel, came up trumps. They put me up free of charge for the night, gave me a bottle of Scotch to help me sleep and contacted Ben to come and see me. He had walked into the Wheatsheaf bar ten minutes after it had happened and, of course, the barmaid told him it was two chaps asking after him, but he had no idea who it could be until now. We had a sombre Saturday evening, slowly getting drunk.

Sunday morning after breakfast I set off home with Nobby's belongings in a white plastic bag on the passenger seat, dreading the meeting with Sylvia, and it was a long while before I could go to sleep at night without seeing Nobby's face ...

The old Wheatsheaf, once the favourite watering hole of White Helmet Display Team members and Nobby's 'Waterloo.'

The Team

Back in 1957 I finished my trade training and got made up officially, where-upon my pay increased to £4 10s 6d per week - I didn't know what to do with it all! My posting came up on the squadron office notice board: 727 Hancox HWG CPL to the Royal Signals Motor Cycle Display Team; someday I'll find out how it was managed, because better blokes that me never made it! I can only think that as The Team used Triumph 500cc twins financed by Triumph, and I worked there, a certain amount of influence was brought to bear. I didn't think that the British Army could be bought, but I reckon it was on this occa-sion — how else could you explain my luck?

The display team was about 35 strong in all, with 21 actual riders, the remainder being ramp men, the hardworking guys who laid out the arena at the beginning of each show, travelled in the back of the Bedford three-tonner and were the backroom boys without whom there would have been no shows at all.

Practising the rides — the opening, middle and closing, was usually carried out on the loose gravel surface of the parade square. Until each rider knew his position completely, at any point, in any ride, all practice was undertaken at half-speed so that it gave him the chance to look towards his opposite number and keep in perfect position, which was of paramount importance. The set piece rides had to have symmetry to look good; in other words your partner had to be exactly opposite you, (a mirror image) at the other end of the arena. When you converged at the centre, crossing right-hand to right-hand, you knew you would miss each other — not by much, but at least you missed! With all riders acknowledging the right-hand to right-hand rule, by and large, there were no nasty pile-ups in the arena centre which, at the Royal Tourna-ment in Earls Court, could be very embarrassing.

When you knew the rides backwards, inside-out and in your sleep, then - and only then - were they performed at proper speed on grass. I say on grass because, with the exception of Earls Court where the indoor arena was covered in peat, all the season's displays were at summer county shows and the like where the arenas were all outside and of grass, usually newly mown (some well-meaning individual would cut it in the belief that short grass was better for us to perform on. In fact, riding on newly mown grass was almost as bad as riding on ice!). Upon arriving at a venue, we would casually walk around the riding arena just to see how the lie of the land was for the no-handed tricks.

During pre-season training, carried out on Matchless G3L machines, each display team member was required to learn how to ride backwards. Not only did this sharpen up your riding ability, but it was advantageous should any member suffer injury during a performance, a substitute on a backwards riding trick could be smoothly slotted in, thus causing no undue disruption to the format of the show.

To get acquainted with backwards riding, it's first of all best to put the bike on the back stand, then climb on sitting backwards on the handlebars or headstock, with your feet on the footrests. Your left hand now has to work the throttle backwards and your right hand the clutch. Assuming that the bike is running (ticking over), you have to master feeding in the clutch, whilst at the same time opening the throttle to take up the drive. Thinking back, I would liken it to having to get used to changing gear with the wrong foot when riding a Japanese motorcycle after being used to an British one. After you had come to terms with the backwards throttle and clutch, you had to learn to do it on the move! With the bike off its stand and the engine running, you would sit on it in the prescribed manner and, with first gear engaged and two helpers holding on to each side of the rear carrier to keep you upright, off you would go. The cardinal rule when learning to ride backwards is when you start to feel yourself fall, increase speed a little and steer into the way you are falling, which I know sounds odd but it does work, I assure you, and with lots of practice you can even set the throttle once on the move and ride backwards no-handed. The really proficient riders could speed off, changing up through the gears and whizz around the arena at speeds of 40 to 50 miles an hour.

All the individual or big composite tricks were practised on the football pitch beside the approach road to the camp for the reason that, should anything go wrong and you fell off whilst performing tricks like the 'Taxi' or 'Six bike fan,' you landed on something softer than tarmac covered in gravel. Sometimes we would even go over the road to Deverell Barracks and practise on the engineers' pitch if ours was in use.

The old stagers, or previous year's team members, whose job it was to train us and pass on their knowledge before being demobbed, would show off occasionally and demonstrate how it really should be done. You would watch them and think "I'll never be able to do that!" — but you did! A certain amount of animosity was shown towards me by the old stagers who had made it on their riding capabilities alone; but after they'd seen my bike and I'd sorted out some of their own bikes that had problems, we all seemed to settle down okay.

As a matter of fact, we had a team reunion in 1988, 30 years after our demob, and held it at the Unicorn Hotel in Ripon during a weekend in May. All 30-odd members of the team turned up, with the exception of a chap called Frazer, who we heard had died some years earlier. During this reunion - which went on for the weekend - I spoke to one of the old stagers who had made my first few weeks in the team uncomfortable, to say the least. His name was Lofty Holman (Lofty because he was big: you didn't argue with him). On

The Unicorn Hotel, another favourite with the 'Team' members and the 1988 reunion venue.

Tales of Triumph & Meriden

The 'Six Bike Fan.' The author is third from the left, bottom row (riding). There were no fixings or braces in this trick, all six bikes and fifteen men were free and on their own. The pressure on the riders' shoulders was almost unbearable.

the Sunday I said to him " Lofty, you never liked me — why?" His reply was "I did like you, but you needed to know you weren't God's gift to the team!" We laughed, had another drink and went in for Sunday lunch, which Maureen and David had put on for us.

Due to the petrol shortage we confined our displays to this country, whereas in later years the White Helmets, as they came to be known, travelled the world. We had good times though, because we could ride the team bikes on the road to shows, whereas in later years they had to be transported with the team members following in a coach. We did many shows around the country, riding from show to show on routes planned by our team captain, John Montague, and generally staying overnight in nearby Army barracks. In Scotland we stayed in Dreghorn Barracks and some Army camp in Aberdeen. In those days — 1957 — there wasn't much traffic on the road and motorcycling was a pleasure, and never more so than when riding up through Scotland past the Lochs of Lomond and Ness. During this time I scrounged a bit of leave between shows during a rest period back at Ripon to go home and marry my Gloria.

Demob couldn't come soon enough but it was still a good way off, so we kept on religiously marking off the dates on the calendar stuck inside our locker doors. An old soldier's saying was "Roll on death — demob's too far away!"

After the rest periods we'd set off in convoy again for the next designated area where the shows were to be performed. Sometimes it was a regimental show somewhere, or even the Bath Searchlight Tattoo! Maybe Edinburgh or

Performing an impromptu trick along the front at Meriden.

the Malvern Showground, within the shadow of the famous hills, for the famous Malvern Three Counties Show. We even did one at the Triumph Gala Day, performing on the playing fields at the back of the factory.

At the start of the season, we'd all been practising on the G3L Matchless models, right up to our visit to Meriden to collect the new twins. This was always an occasion and the workers would all come out to watch while the new bikes were tried out, either on the drive along the front of the factory or on the front lawn. The Speed Twin and Watsonian aluminium bodied single-seater sidecar wasn't ready, however; this would have to be collected the following week when Watsonian had completed modifications: a small aperture to peer through at the front on the underside of the sloping sidecar 'nose' and a quickly detachable sidecar wheel. The sidecar came with no windscreen but had a snap-down tonneau cover.

The Speed Twin was the standard 1957 swinging arm model, but it also had one or two modifications, the main one being adaptation for remote steering. We affixed to the nearside corner of the front-stand a plate, into which was mounted a ball-joint coupling. This crossed to the underside of the sidecar body and connected to a tiller bar assembly bolted on the chassis, with the tiller bar itself inside the sidecar. Our smallest man, Charlie Theobald, could lie down inside the sidecar head first, be covered by the tonneau so that he couldn't be seen and, peering through the aperture, steer the outfit!

We also required a secondary speed control as well as the standard throttle on the bike. This was accomplished by fitting a one-into-two throttle cable incorporating the high-performance twin carburettors, chromium-plated junction box that was used when anyone wanted to fit twin carburettors on their

Tales of Triumph & Meriden

Collecting the new bikes from Meriden in 1957. The author is third from the right.

Discussing the merits of the 'remote' combo with motorcycle journalist, Vic Willoughby. Charlie Thoebold's 'peephole' can be clearly seen at the front of the sidecar.

T100 or T110 for racing. This not only allowed the combo to be ridden using the twistgrip normally, but also by connecting the other cable to a lever inside the sidecar mounted on the tiller-bar, Charlie could control the outfit's speed as well. It was quite nice to ride really; the Speed Twin didn't make too hard a job of pulling the sidecar.

The quickly-detachable sidecar wheel was relatively simple to operate as well: a spring-loaded, fork-ended plunger which, when pulled by Charlie, would disengage from a milled slot in the sidecar wheel stub axle, thereby allowing the wheel to be pulled out of its mounting arm and thrown away. These were all going to be put to good use, making the riderless motorbike and sidecar trick one of the show highlights!

I could ride combo pretty good, so Captain Montague ordered me to draw a one-way rail warrant to Coventry where I hopped on a bus and went home. As JRW 405 was back at camp I had to get to Meriden somehow, so I asked one of my pals to run me over there on his 500cc AJS Springtwin. Alex dropped me off at the gatehouse on the main drive and waved cheerio as I went into the main factory, through the rubber swing doors and into the main finishing shop. I'd got my Barbour suit on and was carrying my white helmet with its Signals crest emblazoned on the front. I suppose I stuck out a bit as I walked through the factory and ribald remarks sprang from either side. "What's the matter? Can't stay away from the bloody place or something?" or "What's the

The author performing 'Backward Threes' with Ken Bailey (centre) and 'Scotty' Christie (right). Note Christie's left eye which was badly cut during the previous trick.

matter, then, diddums lose his bikey-wikey?" All pretty good-natured I suppose and somewhat expected.

When I got to the repair shop, the chaps were all interested in how things were and I got a mug of tea made for me by old Arthur the labourer whilst Reg got the combo out. It looked a super job, with the bike in the classic Amaranth Red and the sidecar in polished aluminium. It really was an eye catcher! Reg gave me a rundown on the dual controls, but they required no explanation as they'd been fitted at the team's request. After finishing my tea I said so long to every one and rode the combo home.

Not being tied down to time I spent the day with Gloria and at about teatime set off for Ripon, following my usual route. This was a smashing run back in 1958 as there was so little traffic on the road compared with today. I used to head out of Coventry, through Ansty, Shilton, Sharnford and into Leicester, round the ring road (although it wasn't called the ring road then, it just skirted round the city centre and was designated A46). Out along the A46 towards

Newark, then left, off to Gunthorpe, Lowdham, coming out on to the A614 Nottingham/Bawtry Road. I'd follow that up through Ollerton and Clumber Park, finally getting to Ranskill, Blythe and Bawtry, where I took the Doncaster road. Straight through Donny, between the football ground and the racecourse and out on to the old A1. Then a straight run up through Wetherby, Boroughbridge and, at Kirby Hill, turn left for the last few miles into Ripon. All in all, I suppose it was about 146 to150 miles which generally took about three hours of steady riding, with no stops, to cover.

There was a very good transport cafe just on the hill going out of Bawtry towards Doncaster that Nobby and I used to sometimes stop at in the early hours of the morning, on our way back to camp after a weekend at home. Obviously, we'd spend as long at home as we could, me leaving Gloria at about 11 o'clock at night and riding over to Nobby's, where his mum would make me a cup of cocoa while he got his kit on; then off we'd set, usually at around midnight. Nobby would ride and I'd be pillion as far as the Avro cafe at Bawtry, where we'd have a big mug of tea and a round of thick buttered toast piled with baked

beans — all for one and threepence (less than 7p) On the run from Bawtry to Ripon I'd ride JRW 405 and reach camp at about 4am, which would give us a couple of hours' kip before having to get up and start the week.

The old Avro Cafe, located on the Doncaster road heading out of Bawtry. It was a favourite stop-off for soldiers on their way back to Ripon or Catterick after weekend leave.

The combination trick always went down well, although there was one occasion when it went down too well with embarrassing results. The combo ride came on twice in the display: the first time with Charlie Theobald secreted in the sidecar and the rider going along no-handed reading a newspaper or book and Charlie doing the steering and controlling the speed. The bike would then turn sharply (Charlie again) and the rider make a big show of falling off. Charlie was now away, going a bit faster, with fallen rider running after the 'runaway' combo, shouting and waving his arms about. Now, one of Charlie's favourite tricks was to head straight at the crowd around the side of the arena (he'd usually target someone and steer straight at them, swerving at the absolute last second). This time he'd chosen a rather amply upholstered older lady sitting in a fold-up wood and canvas chair. As the supposedly runaway combo headed towards her she started to struggle to get out of the chair, but to no avail as she was wedged in too tightly, so she tried to stand up, only to fall over backwards, chair and all! Of course, the crowd went wild with ecstatic applause, thinking it was all part of the act! The show organizers, however, received a complaint. To make amends we all paraded in front of her and apologized for giving her a fright which she took with good grace, calling us "a load of young buggers." We laughed for days over it, but Charlie was more careful and didn't target any more fat old ladies in canvas chairs.

On one of our trips we passed close to Coventry. It was about Sunday lunchtime, I remember, when I saw Monty (Captain Montague) signal that he wanted to speak to me. He rode at the front of the convoy on the Speed Twin with Charlie Theobald in the chair and I, as the fitter, rode at the very rear in case anyone dropped out with mechanical problems (not that they ever did). I worked my way up and rode close alongside him so that he could shout his message. "You live around here, Corporal Hancox, don't you?" "Yes sir, not too far." He shouted "Do you think your Mum could fix us up with a cup of tea at short notice?" "Of course, she'd be glad to" I yelled back. He signalled me to lead the way.

Oh dear! It was now about two o'clock on a Sunday afternoon and I felt sure Mum and Dad would be having their usual doze after Sunday lunch. They were in for a surprise to say the least! By the time we arrived at my home address, 68 Hen Lane, Coventry, it was after 2.30 and I could imagine all the neighbours having a quiet hour in their easy chairs as we roared down the lane and parked outside my house. With a lot of throttle blipping (remember, these bikes were 500 twins on straight-through pipes with no silencers), the bikes were lined up and all the riders shut-off at a wave of command from the Captain. By this time, people were at windows and doors - my Auntie Trixie two doors away, my Nan three doors away and finally my Mum and Dad. Well, there were twenty-two of us in my house for Sunday tea, blokes all over the place. Auntie Trixie and my Nan brought out two huge enamel teapots and from somewhere else loads of sandwiches, it was all go! My Dad, I seem to remember, was sitting in the corner with Captain Montague, engaged in earnest conversation and drinking Navy rum. It was a hell of a party and by the time we were ready to go poor old Monty had to be helped into the sidecar and Charlie rode the bike! With a vague wave of his hand as a start-up signal, we all fired up together. The noise was shattering. Two of the lads even gave an impromptu backwards riding and standing in the saddle display, up and down the lane before we finally moved off. In later years, my Mum told me the neighbours thought it was great and talked of it for ages. Happy memories ...

I mentioned earlier the Malvern Three Counties Show as one of the places we gave displays. This was indeed a splendid showground — level, nicely mown a few days previously and with no unexpected humps. Upon arrival we usually walked over the area, studying the ground rather like a golfer does before attempting a putt, to determine whether there were any bumps hidden in the grass that would upset a no-handed trick. If you were sitting on the handlebars facing backwards with your arms outstretched and had two other chaps on the bike with you, the last thing you wanted was to hit a bump with the

Willie doing a solo 'Forwards Jimmy'.

front wheel!

We undertook a show at a small village later on in the season, somewhere near Hull I think, called Thorgumbold on Ryehill. When we arrived, we nearly fell off our bikes with laughter at the state of the field for, not only did it slope from top to bottom, it had huge ridges running across it! This was going to make things very difficult, especially for the Taxi, Tableaux and Six Bike Fan. We usually kept the speed at between 10 and 12mph in the no-handed tricks, but because of the slope we found that on the return run our speed was up around 30mph as we were going downhill!

The Malvern Showground was nothing short of perfect for our displays over the three-day period that we were there. We were contracted to do one show in the late morning and another after lunch, so when you had checked your bike over and made sure your kit was spick-and-span, you could really do what you wanted. We usually had some sort of tent or large marquee at our disposal, so it was great to get out of your 'blues' and stretch out for a kip. Riding all over the country made you tired and the ordinary British soldier in the Fifties usually made a bit of a kip his number one priority when and if the chance came along.

The young 'Willie.' Les Williams performing the 'Tableaux' ride at the Command Central ground, Catterick. It took strength and skill to keep straight and level with ten men aboard.

We were billeted at Malvern Barracks for the three nights, and I remember the NAAFI there was one of the best I'd ever been in, having a splendid food selection but, better still, genuine scrumpy. In the evening, after getting the bikes put away and cleaning and pressing our blues for the following day's shows, we'd go for a walk to the NAAFI for a drink and something to eat. One evening we were early and, just as we walked in, the shutter-blind rolled up to reveal row upon row of pint glasses, all filled to the brim with this queer-looking stuff that appeared to have bits floating on it! At something like 6d (two-and-a-half new pence) a glass, it went down a treat with all of us, especially with a big plateful of egg, chips, sausage and beans!

Charlie Theobald reckoned the stuff wasn't all it was cracked up to be and after about three pints decided he'd go to the bar for his fourth, saying something like "This stuff's only like pop; I could drink it all night!" With that he tried to get up off his chair. The three of us — Mike Furness, Ken Bailey and I - sat looking at him, wondering why he was still sitting there, when he said "My bloody legs won't move!" There was a definite hint of panic in all of us, and with extreme effort we managed to walk outside into the evening air without falling over or making prats of ourselves. Strange thing was, it didn't really affect your head or even make you feel as if there was anything wrong — it was only when you tried to walk! I reckon the girl behind the NAAFI counter must have thought we were right pillocks!

The other show that was really good and full of atmosphere was the Bath Searchlight Tattoo which went on for a full week. The showground was in the centre of Bath and all elements of the armed forces took part: for instance, the RAF had dog teams, the armoured blokes took a couple of the latest tanks (at that time I think they were Centurions), we were there, and there was an American Air Force band. These chaps were something else! We'd never seen blokes in beautiful gaberdine uniforms, chrome-plated helmets, white cravats, gloves and gaiters before. The music was all Glenn Miller stuff, played on the march — they had the crowd in raptures, night after night. Seeing those chaps march, doing their fancy step routine, never losing the strict tempo and playing *In the Mood*, *Little Brown Jug* and several other classics has always stuck in my mind.

We had a couple of big marquees where we could get our heads down and we shared our huge tent, with a partition down the centre, with the Yanks - as we called them, rather disrespectfully. They were a great bunch of blokes, quite a few of whom were motorcyclists and very interested in our bikes and the tricks we were doing on them every afternoon and evening.

I must say the evening shows were the most spectacular with the bikes flashing and glinting under the huge arc-lights that illuminated the arena, and when the American Air Force band marched, the lights reflecting off the chrome helmets and instruments was dazzling. The showground was sort of sunken, below the level of the main top road, and all along the head of the arena was what appeared to be a castle wall, topped by battlements. I seem to remember on the two sides the ground sloped upwards, forming a natural sort of amphitheatre which echoed the bikes' exhaust noise to good effect. We played to packed audiences every performance and soon struck up a friendship with the Yanks.

During the evening, whilst lying awake in the tent, we could hear the band members on the other side of the partition playing poker. Sometimes the game would go on all night and they'd still be playing when we got up the next morning! One chap lost his Volkswagen Beetle, then played right through the night until he won it back again!

Two or three Americans owned Triumphs and wanted to know what it was like to perform on grass, doing the various tricks and co-ordinated rides, so we organised a little display one morning. We got a band member on the pillion of each bike and proceeded to go through the opening, middle and closing rides. We even got them on some of the backwards tricks which tickled them no end. All in all, we made some good friends that week and I, in fact, stayed in contact with one of them for a couple of years after my demob.

Back in Ripon we all went to The Black Dog for a well-deserved booze-up — after all, the shows had all finished and several of us would be leaving soon to make way for fresh members to be trained to replace us. We had several days at Ripon, getting the Triumphs ready to go back to Meriden where they'd be overhauled by the service repair department and made as new again, ready for next year when the whole lot would start all over again.

When the season ended, I still had a couple of months to go to finish my time, so I got a posting as a driver in the War Office on the Thames embankment. It was a cushy posting and being in barracks at Hounslow and driving to the War Office each day seemed almost like going to work normally. There were two drivers per shift to take the messages that came in on the teleprinters to their various destinations in and around London - the Admiralty, the Air Ministry, the various high commissions and so on.

The days dragged by; slowly but surely the great moment was approaching when I would walk out of the gates in civvies and know it was all finished with. I hadn't taken JRW 405 to London, simply because it wasn't as easy to get weekends off, but when you did it was very simple to hop on the underground and get a fast train (steam, in those days!) from Euston. I could be home in just over an hour and a half, and with a bus home from the station, two hours was about it.

My demob date coincided with some sort of big inspection by the Colonel-in-Chief of the regiment. As was customary, you had to hand in your kit, getting documents, receipts and chits as they were called, signed all the while until on your last night you were dressed in your civilian clothes with only your bedding to hand in to the QM (Quartermasters stores) the following morning. After some breakfast in the cookhouse, I handed in my mattress, blankets, sheets and pillow and, as I stood outside the QM stores door, thought "That's it, I've nothing left of the Army's." I could go home as soon as I'd seen the Commanding Officer and had the customary "Do you want to sign for another three years, soldier? The Army is a good life, you know, with plenty to offer a young chap!" I thought "Not on your life, old son" but actually found myself saying "No thank you, sir, I have a job and a wife waiting." With that he rose, we shook hands and he wished me luck. As I wasn't wearing a uniform or beret I didn't salute, just turned and walked out of his office, closing the door behind me. It felt really strange, not saluting an officer for the first time in two years! But stranger still was twelve months later when the team came to Meriden and I saw Captain Montague again and I called him "Sir." Funny old world.

'The Taxi.' 22 men on one bike, a standard - apart from extra footrests - TRW 500cc SV Twin. Men climbed aboard as the bike moved around the arena, with the author (front left) and Dave Race (with leg out) being the last two on. Charlie Theobold is on top giving directions to the rider (whose helmet can just be seen!) This world record stood for many years. Tyre pressure for this trick was 70-80psi.

Meriden again!

I'd still got JRW 405 but by now she was looking decidedly worn and tired, to say the least. I reckon a spanner hadn't been near her for two years, and all that time she'd faithfully carried Nobby and me backwards and forwards each weekend. I didn't keep count of the mileage but it must have been pretty high. I did check the consumption once on a run home and it worked out at 70 miles per gallon on Army petrol, which was pretty good.

It was nearing June 1959 when I returned to Meriden to take up a position in the experimental department under Mr Frank Baker, who was then the manager. The foreman was a man called Jack Varlow who sported a huge handlebar moustache, a Londoner who had previously been involved with the development of the AJS Porcupine racer. The chargehand was a small, tubby, grey-haired chap from Kenilworth called Tommy Wallace, who was quite a fearsome old soul really, especially if you didn't do your job properly.

The fitters were Steve 'Pop' Tilley, Dennis 'The Menace' Austin, a younger chap called Alan Gillingham (who later on left to join the Ferguson Formula four-wheel-drive team at Baginton in Coventry), and me, straight out of the Army. There were two road testers: Bert Whatmore, affectionately called Whistle for reasons that will become obvious later on, and the one and only inimitable Percy Tait, or Sam Tait, as we called him.

I can't remember what Dennis Austin was working on, but Alan Gillingham had just put together a 1959 Tiger 110 in the colour of the day which was Silver Grey (Crystal Grey, as it was known later). It had slightly lowered suspension, T100C inverted bars (the little short ones that came out of the nacelle and dropped). It also had the reduced-diameter exhaust pipes into Burgess straight-through silencers which made the most beautiful noise when the motor was pulling hard, as it inevitably was when Perc was on it!

The two most important new things on the motor were, firstly, the introduction of the E3134 inlet camshaft (to run in conjunction with the standard Tiger 110 E3325 cam on the exhaust side) which gave a new valve timing

Meriden again!

(inlet opens 34 degrees, inlet closes 55 degrees, exhaust opens 48 degrees, exhaust closes 27 degrees) and provided the engine with better all-round performance. The second new item was the Delta splayed port cylinder head, which could now take twin 1 1/16 inch bore Amal Monobloc carburettors.

The bike was fearsome on performance, as was soon proved when Percy took it to MIRA (the Motor Industries Research Association proving ground at Lindley near Nuneaton) and lapped the high speed banked circuit at something approaching 130mph!

About this time, Norman Dewis was at the proving ground with, I think, the E-type Jaguar prototype and he and Percy had a bit of a do on the high speed (or Number 1, as it was called) lap with Percy clocking the fastest speed at 132mph! This time stood for quite a long while — years, in fact — because at that sort of speed, when you hit the banking the centrifu-

Young Percy Tait (centre) at Mallory, with a 'secret' works T100 racer. With him are (left) Steve 'Pop' Tilley and Dennis 'The Menace' Austin.

Bert 'Whistle' Whatmore on a photographic stint for the Tiger Cub in 1960. He always was a good-looking so-and-so!

Tales of Triumph & Meriden

Production testers leaving on a run.

The remote float layout on the 1959 T120 Bonneville.

gal force carries you upwards towards the rim, so Percy was actually slowing down for the banking and accelerating off it down the straights. We were quite elated because this was going to be a new model, introduced into the 1959 show line-up as a last minute decision by ET to celebrate the world speed record victory on the Bonneville salt flats in Utah. That's it, Bonneville, the word that was to become virtually a household name, and I had a part in the model's making and preparation.

By this time, the experimental department had outgrown its little space opposite the paint shop and just around the corner from both the spares and service departments, so a brand new extension to the right of the main entrance was built. This sort of balanced the look of the factory from the front, but it partially obscured the service area, my old department. Customers wishing to visit either service or spares departments now had to go round the end of experimental and proceed along a drive formed by the rear wall of the experimental shop and the front of the service and spares departments. There was no real problem with this, not unless the double doors on the front of the new shop were left open on a hot day, when you'd suddenly have a feeling of being stared at and, upon turning round, would find two or three people — customers who had brought their bikes to the service department — staring wide-eyed at everything in the experimental shop. Once a chap even produced a camera from under his riding coat and asked if we minded if he took a few snaps. With the new Bonnie in there, and also one or two bikes with the new duplex frame for the 1960 season, poor old Frank Baker nearly had a fit! After that, we had a screen put up just inside the open doors to conceal us from onlookers but, even then, we did have one cheeky so-and-so take a couple of paces inside and peer round the edge of the screen. Needless to say, after that we mostly kept the door shut.

By now, a third tester had joined us, a nice chap called Stan Jinks. He and Bert (Whistle) Whatmore were mostly on mileage (usually running a bike with a new type of part either in it or on it), whilst Perc was on high speed (and I mean high speed) road testing, putting miles on the Bonnie (or 'The Monster,' as Alan Gillingham and I had christened it).

Perc would arrive at the department at about three minutes past eight and clock in. He only had to come from his farm on the Fillongley Road about one mile into Meriden, then out of the village, up Meriden Hill, down the other side, brake hard and turn into the factory. He reckoned if he walked out of his kitchen as the eight o'clock pips were going on the radio, he'd be in time to clock in and not lose a quarter! Later on, when Percy actually went home on the prototype Bonneville, it wasn't uncommon to see people stand outside, just to listen to the music of

The first duplex frame without secondary cross-bar in 1959 for the 1960 season.

Perc approaching the factory! You could hear him accelerate out of the village, power on up the hill and over the top, then start changing down from 100mph plus to brake for the factory gates. Magic!

Perc would get 400 miles a day in on the Monster by arriving for work at his usual time. Alan and I would check it over, oil, tyre pressures, chains and fuel, finally giving it a wipe over and adjusting the clutch, front brake and so on. Perc would then set off down the newly opened M1 motorway and proceed all the way to the end, promptly turn around and come back again at a high rate of knots, arriving in time for lunch break. (Alan and I usually ate on an early break). We would again check the bike over, getting it up on the trestle, one working either side, to make sure everything was in order. We'd check oils, adjustments again, top up with fuel and have it ready for Perc after he'd finished his meal. After a quick cup of tea, on would go his helmet and off he'd go again on the same run, arriving back in time to clock out and go home on another bike.

This went on for weeks until the Northamptonshire Police complained about his excessive speed through their county. Neither we nor Perc thought any-

Original 1959 single down-tube frame Bonneville, which was nicknamed 'The monster'. Note the Tiger T110 timing cover patent plate.

thing of it until the Bedfordshire Police also complained that he and the Aston Martin testers were racing each other and going through the Luton bends so quickly they were drifting! Perc took no notice, mainly because he was riding one of the fastest things on two wheels and he knew for certain the police had nothing to touch him — but they had other ways. On a morning return run to the factory, Perc was giving it some stick, 'on full noise' as he used to say, when he noticed a conglomeration of vehicles in the distance which appeared to be filing into the nearside lane. When he got closer, he saw that the middle and outside lanes had been coned off, funnelling all the traffic through to the nearside lane only. He told me afterwards he had no idea what was going on until he got closer to the policemen scrutinising the vehicles as they slowly passed by. One of them smiled evilly and pointed directly at him, signalling him to pull over. "Got you at last" the policeman said with a smile. Perc went to court and was fined, which the firm paid. He got off the charge of dangerous driving due to a good lawyer pointing out that he, Perc, was probably as proficient at these high speeds as an ordinary road user would be at a much slower pace.

The new workshop was much larger than the old place and actually had a cellar in which to store bike bits. (In the old workshop we did have a sort of

Meriden again!

Meriden Hill coming out of the village. If Cubs didn't pull 55mph in 4th gear up here, then there was something wrong.

stores to keep prototype engines and bits in, but it took up valuable floor space). The new storeroom was just a large square hole in the concrete floor with a railing around and steps leading down. The hole was big enough to lower a bike through, and to do this we had an electric hoist running along a girder in the roof. It was simple to bring anything up or take anything down; you just placed the sling under the frame of the bike, hooked it up to the hoist and lifted it gently a few inches to ascertain the point of balance. You could then hoist the bike high enough to clear the railing, move it along on its track so that it was over the hole and simply lower away until it stood on its centre-stand on the cellar floor.

The hoist came in for other uses, too. Alan Gillingham was a good joker, as Perc found to his cost one day. There had been some banter going on between them and it ended with Perc throwing a mug of water at Alan, who didn't retaliate immediately. Instead he looked at me, grinned wolfishly and winked. Just before going-home time, Perc had completed his run, had been to the toilets and was standing by the railing around the hole, talking to Stan Jinks and Whistle Whatmore. Alan had prepared the hoist earlier in the afternoon, putting it in the right position and leaving just enough play in the hook and chain, which was hooked over the railing just behind where Perc was standing. Whistling and bustling about, Alan walked up behind the three testers and quickly but gently placed the hook under Perc's riding suit belt, at the same time with his other hand activating the hoist. Poor old Perc! Up he went, kicking and shouting. Alan just left him there, slowly going red in the face. I didn't realise riding suit belts were that strong. We all went home and left Perc dangling. Who let him down we don't know, but he never threw water at Alan again!

After the Bonneville went to the show, the public - and Americans in particular - couldn't get enough of it. We had little or no trouble with it except for the new cylinder heads cracking from the inboard cylinder head bolt holes

Tales of Triumph & Meriden

Looking at the front of Meriden with the new drawing office above the experimental department. The cars belong to service and spares personnel.

through to the valve seats. On the whole, the bike was good because, basically, it was running on the tried and tested T110 chassis. This was very reliable, as Mike 'The Bike' Hailwood and 'Banbury' Danny Storey proved at the 1958 Thruxton 500 miles where they cleaned up.

Framed

The year progressed and I was engaged on testbed work, running a Tiger Cub motor carrying out tests on oil pumps, oil flow rates and pressures. All this time the new duplex frames were being run and, in 1960, they were introduced. The whole 650 range was revamped - not to the liking of some employees, I might add! The Thunderbird and Tiger 110 now came with the rear enclosure, or Bathtub, as we called it, I suppose because it was similar in shape to the old hipbath of bygone days. This made life difficult when you wanted to work on the back end of the bike as it had to be removed first.

The TR6 Trophy and T120 Bonneville were now more sporting, with new duplex frames, gaitered forks, chrome headlamps and sports mudguards and handlebars. They also had new paint schemes. Things appeared okay for a while, then a bad call came from the States from ET who was over there at the time. He said a chap had been killed on a new frame bike during the Big Bear Run (an endurance speed race across desert terrain.) Apparently, after hitting a series of bumps at high speed, his frame fractured through just below the steering head lug on the double-down tubes. He was thrown off and, of course, at the speeds these guys raced at (up to 100mph) was killed. We all knew what was coming; some days later, ET came down the corridor from his office and into experimental, his face as black as thunder and wanting to know why the frame had fractured. No-one could tell him but we knew we had to find out - and quickly.

Frank Baker booked the Belgian Pave circuit at MIRA and I made up a team of four with Percy, Stan and Whistle. We took two bikes straight off the track, a Tiger 110 and a Trophy TR6, which we took it in turns to ride, doing five laps each at speeds of 30 to 35mph. On the first morning, we clocked in as usual, got the two bikes out of the experimental shop, together with the box combo, a beautiful swinging-arm Thunderbird in Burnished Gold. Pop Tilley looked after this, did the servicing, maintenance and generally kept it in superb order. You could honestly jump on it at any time and ride it the length of

Tales of Triumph & Meriden

Stan Jinks on MIRA's 'Belgian Pave' in 1957. The Pave was so vicious at 30-38mph that it even stopped your wristwatch!

the country with no problems at all. It went like a scalded cat but was extremely good on fuel as it was equipped with an SU carburettor. Percy took the box combo with Stan Jinks on the pillion, while Whistle rode the Trophy TR6 and I rode the Tiger 110.

At the end of the first day, with Percy and Whistle taking it in turns to complete five laps each on the Trophy, and Stan and I doing the same on the Tiger 110, we were still fairly chipper and quite full of ourselves when we got back to Meriden. On the second morning after clocking in, Percy took the Trophy TR6 to ride to MIRA with Whistle on the Tiger 110. Stan came with me on the 6T box combo and, being slower than the solos, we set off five or so minutes before the others. We got into Meriden village and turned right at the island proceeding up the Fillongley Road. This was Percy's domain; he had the bends and curves weighed up to a tee and I doubt whether anyone on the face of this planet could catch him along that particular stretch of road. Whistle and Percy always did have ding-dongs along there, but Whistle could never better Percy, no matter what.

On this particular morning, Stan and I were pressing on quite quickly when the two of them flew by us at an incredible speed, Percy in the lead and Whistle right up his exhaust pipe. The shock of them coming by at such a terrific rate made both Stan and I jump. Stan tapped me on the shoulder and yelled in my ear "Mad buggers!" By now we had almost reached Percy's farm and only had to go along the straight and round the wiggly bit, as Perc called it. I was no slouch on a combo, having ridden the display team Speed Twin and sports Watsonian for many miles, but as we came to the end of the straight we must have been a long way behind them. I went into the left-hander with both of us leaning over the box hard, then had to anchor up as quickly as I could, for there on the road was the Tiger 110. Narrowly missing it, we pulled up, at the same time noticing Whistle on his hands and knees in the middle of the road. Jumping off the Thunderbird, Stan and I ran over to him to see if he was alright. We were surprised to see him pound his clenched Barbour-mitted fists on the road and hear him yell at the top of his voice "If he can get round, why the bloody Hell can't I?" After calming him down and getting him back on the bike, we set off to MIRA at a more leisurely pace, only to be greeted by Percy upon our arrival, sitting side-saddle on the TR6, helmet and gloves off, with a grin from ear to ear. "Where the hell have you lot been?" he shouted. Stan and I had to hold on to Whistle very tightly!

Perc was like that. I've never known a man who could ride on ordinary roads like him, except maybe Alex Scobie in his younger years. It was a thrill to see Percy ride on ice or hard-packed snow. I never knew how he did it; after all, I fell off a Cub coming up Meriden hill! One day as we stood having our mugs of tea, Whistle asked Percy "How do you manage to ride so quickly, feet up, on ice and snow?" The Maestro replied "It's easy, you've got to relax, whistle or sing to yourself, but don't tense up." Whistle Whatmore looked at me, I looked at him and we must have read each other's thoughts. "Great, that's the secret. I'll try it." Out on the rutted snow and ice that morning Bert came an awful cropper down Fillongley Road, but he was still whistling when we pulled him out of the hedge!

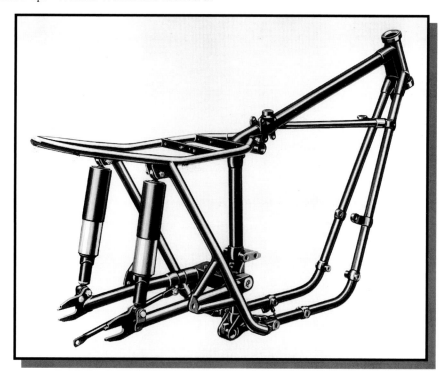

The third day of Pave testing bought upset stomachs, wrist watches that wouldn't work and eyeballs that rattled in their sockets. Frank Baker had picked a speed that would make vibration as bad as possible and it broke the frames: both of them went within two laps of each other after four days. It was obviously time for a major rethink on this new frame ...

As far as we could make out, the forks were flexing the head-lug casting on the single top frame tube and the two smaller diameter down tubes. That was it! So why not put the second cross-bar in as it had been on the earlier single down-tube frames? The new duplex job had only one cross-bar which was allowing the head lug to flex too much, causing the two smaller diameter tubes to fracture where they emerged from the bottom of the head lug casting. Fitting the secondary tube should prevent any flexing and hopefully cure the problem. But we had to be sure, which is where little Dennis

Modified duplex with additional cross-bar, which proved successful, preventing further frame breakages.

Austin came in with his ingenious ideas.

I was to help him on this so, after he'd made a sketch of what he wanted to do, I had to study it and gather material to make it, while he shot off on the experimental box combo to Aston in Birmingham where, apparently, he knew someone who worked in the shunting yards and loco workshops. When he came back he was carrying a locomotive connecting rod from a little shunting loco which was about four-and-a-half feet long, with a big end diameter of some 10 or 11 inches. By now I'd got an RSJ girder and cut it up to arc-weld together in a rectangular frame, which was then rawl-bolted to the cellar floor on rubber anti-vibration mounts. Next, we got dear old Frank Green on his magic lathe to make an eccentric cam that would run inside the big end, which could be oil fed from a drip-feed reservoir. Old Frank Green was a wonder worker; it didn't matter whether you gave him a rough sketch on a fag packet or a proper drawing, he'd turn out a super job every time!

We now fitted some crossmembers to the frame, and on to one of these mounting points for a single phase electric, variable-speed motor. Off its double V belt pulley, we took a drive to a cross-shaft on the other crossmember, running in 'fenner' bearing housings. On this cross-shaft was mounted the eccentric cam and, on that, the conrod. All we had to do now was bolt the frame down to welded-on mounting points, and flexibly connect the other (small) end of the conrod to the frame head lug. We made the cross-shaft mounting on a slider, which we could adjust using a nut and bolt as a fine tuner, to achieve varying amounts of punch to the head lug when the motor was switched on.

It was all devilishly simple, but oh so effective! The new frame ran for days and days with nothing happening to it, so Dennis the Menace tweaked up the adjustment a bit. Crikey, we could feel the floor shaking in the experimental shop and it wasn't long before the office girls in the main building started to complain, too! After a while we did get one frame to go, but we were satisfied that the new double-down tube frame with the added top rail had done the trick. All that remained was for the boss to report it all to ET - didn't envy him that one ...

The time soon came for me to say cheerio to the lads in the experimental shop and move on for a stint in production test.

The Best Motorcycle in the World

A testing time

I had to go down to the finishing shop and report to Mr Sidney Tubb, the man who had initially interviewed me when I first started six years ago. I don't think he remembered me; if he did, he didn't show it.

I had my own riding suit but definitely had to have a new one as it was part of the job. Mr Tubb usually had one or two spare suits in his office, but the ones I tried must have been made for King Kong, because the sleeves were so long they dragged on the floor! "You'd better get yourself off to Belstaff's" he said. "Go and get a works order for one and I'll sign it." I'd already been issued with my two trade plates and I said to him, rather naively, "How do I get there?" He stopped writing, looked up at me and slowly replied "On a motor cycle!" I took this to mean I could just walk into the finishing shop, pick up any new bike, check it over, fit my trade plates, fill it up with petrol and go, and that's what I did! Not wishing to be too pushy I selected a T100A and, wearing my own suit, off I went. (I suppose most young chaps would agree with me that their idea of heaven is where you get to ride brand new Triumphs, straight off the production line — and get paid for it too!) At last, I thought, as I accelerated up the road and breasted the top of Meriden hill, I'm one of the legendary black-jacketed testers. It shouldn't take me long to get to Stone in Staffordshire on this baby, I thought, as I whistled down Meriden Hill, so full of myself that I didn't notice another black-suited figure hurtling down the hill behind me. I'd got just about two thirds of the way down the hill, humming to myself, when someone pinched my bum and I nearly fell off the bike! It was Percy, the rotten sod. He'd seen me set off from the works yard, just as he'd come out of the experimental on a Bonnie, and given chase. He'd closed on me very fast then coasted to sneak up undetected so that he could carry out his dastardly deed. He'd got me back for the hoist trick; I wondered what he had up his sleeve for Alan Gillingham?

Back at the finishing shop, resplendent in my new suit, I was instructed in the rudimentals by chief tester Jimmy Brown. There were, counting myself, twelve testers and each chap tested twelve bikes a day; thirteen, counting your going-home bike (you were allowed to go home on a different, brand new Triumph every night - WOW!) The route we used was: left out of the factory, up to the top of Meriden Hill, down hill and through Meriden village to the island, left at the island and down to the bottom of Hampton Lane, locally known as the Meriden Mile. We were required to ride sensibly at all times, noting problems — if any — and then do a full bore run down the mile to ensure everything was functioning correctly at speed. Contrary to popular belief, you can ride a bike flat-out with only 10 or 11 miles on the clock, provided you do it sensibly and without making the unit labour too much.

About three-quarters of the way down the mile you could ease back and, at the bottom, turn into Cornets End Lane, putting the bike on its stand and letting it tick over. We generally set the carbs, checked for any problems, oil leaks or whatever, switched off whilst we had a fag (those of us who didn't smoke just had a breather) and then proceeded at a medium pace back to the factory to complete the test report card. This was then tucked behind a knee-pad rubber and the bike was pushed down to the rectification section (or knacker gang, as they were known) for the timing, tappets and chains to be readjusted. When that was done, the fuel would be drained and the bike cleaned ready for despatch. Oh yes, when the bike came off the production line it was fitted with slave exhaust pipes (old pipes used for testing purposes only). Once it was cleaned, the new pipes were fitted and it was ready for despatch.

To be a Triumph tester in the summer was marvellous, but, in the winter, not so good. You still had to complete your quota, irrespective of the weather: I used to get home in the evening sopping wet and Gloria would somehow have to get my riding suit dry for the next day. It wasn't long before the factory authorised the supply of the new Belstaff suit made out of a different type of material, which had a quilted lining and electrically-welded instead of stitched seams. These were a 100 per cent improvement on the earlier Belstaff type suit of waxed cotton, but they went so stiff in the winter and we were all walking around like Michelin men. Well, you can't have everything.

One of the things that Jimmy Brown the chief tester didn't officially tell me was that all the testers visited Fred's Cafe on the Fillongley Road twice a day — once in the morning at about 10.15am and again in the afternoon at about 3.30pm. Fred was a nice old character (a bit like Les Dawson, the comedian) with a permanently mournful expression on his face, but nice nevertheless. That cafe was an inviting place on a cold, wet winter's day, especially in the afternoon when you'd been out in it all day and were getting to the end of your tether. Percy and Whistle were on mileage from the experimental and shouldn't have been in there at all! On one occasion, one of the production testers was sitting in the steamed-up cafe, cradling a hot mug of tea in his hands, when he said to Whistle "Why don't you put the bike on its centre-stand, stick it in fourth and set the throttle? You'll be clocking up miles even while you're in here." Whistle thought this a good idea and the next day, during the afternoon break, he came in with a huge grin on his face, gave us the thumbs-up and ordered his mug of tea. When he came to the table and sat down, we asked him what he was so pleased about. "I've done what you suggested," he said "it's so simple, I can't think why it isn't done more often." "That's why!" said one of the blokes, as Whistle's bike shot off across the carpark and disappeared into the hedge! The vibration of the running engine had moved the bike along on its stand until the rear wheel had contacted the ground and propelled the bike forward.

Whistle dropped the idea completely whilst we, over our mugs of tea, started designing little gadgets on bits of paper, incorporating washing machine motors, speedo cables and suchlike, which would enable miles to be clocked even when the bike was stationary. Nothing ever came of it, although it was a grand idea: a row of bikes at the back of the cafe, all with their speedos connected to these little motors and the miles just mounting up, while we sat in the warm.

By now, it was 1961 and the bikes were coming off the tracks thick and fast because Triumph was riding on the crest of a wave, selling anything we could make. The Bonnevilles going to the States were in different trim to the home market bikes, having high-rise bars and the beautiful noise-making short Burgess silencers. They were a joy to ride, with 'punch' from nothing all the way up the rev range. I derived as much enjoyment from riding the more mundane models, however, such as the Tiger Cub, the Tiger 100A, Speed Twin 5TA and the somewhat gutless 3TA, or Twenty One, as it was known at first. There was a cracking little Cub on the go at that time called the T20SL, which had energy transfer ignition, a 9 to 1 compression ratio, a 376 Amal Monobloc carb fitted with remote float bowl and the higher performance R camshaft. It was the Sports Cub, which had larger wheels, forks and separate headlamp and was finished in the same colours as the Bonneville. It was called, by some people, the baby Bonnie because it went so well. To test it I partnered up with

One of the quickest Cubs ever: the 1960 T20SL with energy transfer ignition, 9:1 CR, sports camshaft and remote float Amal carburettor.

A very nice 1961 T20SL, again, with 'E.T.' ignition but flat roadster bars and standard tyres.

a chap named Joe Price, nicknamed Sooty. It was always better to ride with someone, just in case anything did go wrong with a bike, as your partner could ride back to the factory for you and summon help. It never happened to me, though. I never ever had a bike go sick on test. There was one chap who rode Cubs all the while and liked them so much he wouldn't give a thank you to ride any other model!

The police bikes of the day were 6T Thunderbirds with a boost switch in the nacelle top which, when pulled, connected the alternator output wires to supply twelve volts instead of the standard six. This was to keep the battery fully charged when the bikes were ridden slowly, escorting a wide load, or on other escort duties, with their blue flashing lights, headlights and radios on. The bikes usually had the letter 'W' stamped behind the engine number to denote high output electrics.

The Thunderbird was normally finished in Charcoal Grey, a rather dowdy colour, and the Police forces expressed a wish for higher visibility colours to be tried. A decision was made on high, between fleet sales, publicity and production departments to take twelve bikes off the track, strip off the painted parts and put them through the paint shop again to have them refinished in a new brilliant white, later to be called 'Motorway White.' When the knacker gang put the bikes together, they really did look splendid in their new white livery.

The publicity department wanted a nice picture of all the bikes; not a static shot with them lined up on their stands but mobile, being ridden. The obvious place to do this was down the Hampton Lane, so all of us testers were told to take a bike each and proceed down the mile. We met the suited gentlemen halfway down, who then requested Jimmy Brown to lead off, with the rest of us as close behind the bike in front as possible. This all seemed straightforward enough, and Jimmy said we'd go to the bottom end of the mile, turn around and come back up at dead on 30mph, as close as possible, keeping our front tyre one or two inches from the rear number plate of the bike in front, which would enable the photographer to get a super shot of us all in line astern.

Now old Jimmy Brown, the chief tester, was nicknamed Clapper, but quite why, no-one knew. Bill Letts, another of my friends, suggested it was because he never applied the brakes — he always clapped the anchors on. We got to the bottom of the mile, turned round and gently accelerated up the mile, get-

A 1963 6T Police Thunderbird.

ting it as tight as possible. We approached the little knot of people at a steady 30mph, so tight I'd actually kissed the rear number plate of Sooty's bike in front with my front tyre on two occasions. What happened next I don't really know, except someone from that little group on the side of the road wasn't satisfied with something or other, because they stepped out, putting up their hand. Clapper put on the brakes and we all bit the dust! There were bits of bikes and blokes all over the road, some of us incapable through laughing so much - two chaps were in the ditch, just lying there laughing! Fortunately, the bikes - despite broken headlamps, rear-lights and screens, and scratched and dented panels and petrol tanks - were still ridable, so we got them back to the factory, lined them up outside, looked at them, shrugged our shoulders and

Tales of Triumph & Meriden

The white Police bikes, after rebuild, on the second photographic run along the newly-opened A45.

Some consider this the finest Bonneville ever made; the 1962 model is certainly the most sought-after in the 1990s.

650 c.c. TRIUMPH BONNEVILLE 120 (T120)

650 c.c. TRIUMPH BONNEVILLE 120

(T120/R)

carried on with testing bikes like we should. As someone remarked "We're not bloody film stars, anyway, are we?"

I don't know what happened to the publicity chaps, maybe ET had them shot at dawn, because there were no more pictures taken that day. Later on a shorter line of five or six riders, each on a newly-painted white Police 6T, had their photograph taken from the top of an embankment on the just-opened by-pass section of the A45.

One of the nicest models to come off the line in 1961 was the American TR6R, which was equipped with separate downswept exhaust pipes, the short Burgess straight-through silencers and, of course, the obligatory high-rise West Coast handlebars. Fitted with only one Amal Monobloc carburettor instead of the twin Amals the Bonnie had, this bike was a real pleasure to ride. We always thought that a nicely set-up TR6 was as quick as a Bonneville and lots nicer to ride anyhow!

Towards the end of 1962 we started to experience piston noise problems and also timing gear howl and whine. It was unusual to get both, as timing gears either clattered from being too loose in mesh or whined from being too tight. To have gears doing both meant there were problems on the manufacturing side with the gear-forming Sykes machine. Pretty soon we were rejecting nearly all the 650 twins tested but, with no discernible improvement in the

The American version of the 1962 T120. With its short Burgess silencers it made a beautiful noise.

93

Tales of Triumph & Meriden

A view of the Triumph yard. The entrance to the finishing shop is on the right and the works canteen (with porch) on the left. The machines pictured are 1961 6T Police 650s.

new batch of gears being made and fitted, we were still not 'passing off' the reworked rejected bikes. It came as a bit of a shock, therefore, to arrive for work one Monday morning and find the sea of rejected machines had all been mysteriously passed off over the weekend by persons unknown. This was the first time I personally encountered the get-the-bikes-out-at-all-costs brigade and to say the testers were teed off with it was a bit of an understatement. I have always maintained that when road testers were done away with and replaced by new-fangled rolling roads, the 'bum-on-the-seat' feeling was lost which led in turn to a decline in standards.

The quality of our jokes on unsuspecting office girls had not declined, however, and the irrepressible Eddie D had somehow obtained an absolutely awful-looking large black spider with huge hairy legs. It was a dead one, of course, but nevertheless it made me shudder to look at it. During the morning tea-break, we all looked on in wonderment as he carefully tied it to a length of black cotton and weighted it with a small nacelle screw nut (the thing must have been three-quarters of an inch across and the body of it completely hid the nut). Each day, just before 12.30, the office girls would walk down through the main finishing shop towards the double rubber doors that led down to the yard outside and the works canteen. Eddie, who was sitting on a bike, had flung the spider's corpse, weighted with the nut, over one of the beams directly above the main gangway, carefully letting the spider down to eye

level and knotting the cotton off at that length around the handlebar of the bike. We all watched in gleeful anticipation as he pulled the spider up again out of sight and then sat there with an innocent expression on his face.

At exactly at 12.30 the finishing bell went for lunchbreak and we heard the gang of office girls, chattering and tripping down the main gangway between the rows of new bikes. Eddie timed it perfectly. All he had to do was relax his forefinger and thumb and the spider dropped to the extent of the length of cotton under its own weight. It seemed to descend quite slowly and just hung there: there was an almighty scream as the few girls at the front of the little bunch saw it - then pandemonium! Eddie laughed so much he fell backwards off the bike and became wedged between it and the next bike in line. It took all three of us to lift him up because we were nearly helpless, too, but that afternoon Mr Sidney Tubb received a visit from the office supervisor demanding retribution.

One friend we testers encountered quite often, when out on the test run, worked for another Coventry company, Jaguar Cars. Dick was the Jaguar service department tester and he used the A45 from Browns Lane where the main Jaguar manufacturing plant was situated, up past Triumph Motorcycles, over the top of Meriden Hill and on down through the village. Here he turned left, as we did on the bikes, to head down the Meriden Mile.

On the day in question, three of us had carried out a fast run down to the bottom of the Mile on American Bonnevilles, running on high compression 11 to 1 pistons, straight-through exhaust systems and big 1 3/16 inch bore twin carburettors. The bikes were destined for American speedway or dirt oval racing as they had no front brakes and the spokes laced straight on to a small flanged wheel hub with no brake drum. These things were very quick indeed, with searing acceleration and a very harsh intractable sort of power that came in with a bang halfway up the rev range.

Proceeding back up the Mile at a slow pace, we usually stopped in the layby for a quick roll-up and a check over of the bikes to make sure everything functioned okay. It was while we sat smoking that the British Racing Green D-type Jaguar pulled up and out clambered Dick in his white, slightly dirty 'cow-gown.' As there was no door on this beautiful little projectile, poor old Dick had to ease himself up and almost fall out backwards! A couple of us helped him as he grumbled "I'm too old for this bloody, silly game!" The motor on the D-type was still running at a very fast tickover as Dick undid the fastenings and lifted the complete front upwards and forwards. There lay the most gorgeous engine with three of the biggest SU carburettors I've ever seen. "Two-inchers" said Dickie as he tweaked the link bar and the engine howled like something alive. With expertise that can only come from years of experience, he tuned and set the three big carbs so that the engine now ran more slowly, but with a beautiful, deep, burbling noise coming from the exhaust. With a final tweak, Dickie blipped the throttle and then reached into the cockpit and switched off.

My friend, Bill Letts, said "God, Dick, that's a beautiful bit of kit, you'd have to be well-heeled to afford one. Who owns it?" "The Duke of Kent" said Dick. "Pull the other one, you old bugger" said Bill. "That's the truth," said Dick, "it's come in to have the small 2.4 engine taken out and the 3.8 put in." We just stood in silence, drawing deeply on our Golden Virginia roll-ups and gazing in silent appreciation at the beautiful piece of engineering laying there, still and silent, but with that smell of newness when hot. "Well," said Dick, stubbing out his cigarette, "must get back, his nibs will be waiting." "Last one back is a sissy!" said Bill as we pulled on our helmets. By now Dick had managed to shoehorn himself into the D-type and, with a stab on the starter button (which, incidentally was the exact same Lucas item that acted as the cut-out button on nacelle/magneto sparked Triumphs), the Jag burst into life. Firing up all three Bonnevilles together with the noise of the D-type was ear-splitting, and as Dick was in front of us in the layby, we graciously waved him off first. We needn't have bothered! The power-to-weight ratio of that little green rocket must have been fantastic because Dick, with an airy wave, proceeded up the remaining two thirds of the Meriden Mile, struggling to keep the thing from breaking sideways with the awesome acceleration.

Try as we might to keep up, we were absolutely left for dead on the run all the way to the island. We caught Dick up going through the village but as we were on straight-throughs and Arthur, the village bobby, had already had one or two complaints from the residents, we kept the throttle off until we hit the bottom of the hill where Dick promptly did his disappearing act again. What a wonderful car: it was the only time I was really envious and wished I was a tester at a factory other than Triumph!

The Tina

About this time three testers, Eddie among them, were seconded to do some mileage on the dreaded automatic 98cc Tina scooter, as penance for the 'dead spider' incident. The usual run was to Banbury, Bourton-on-the-Water and back again, quite a stint on a motorbike like that, especially if you were on the large side, as two of the blokes were. The third rider just happened to be small, so on the straight he would ease himself off the seat and crouch down on the running boards behind the front panel, thus giving a better slipstream through the air and allowing a higher speed. This was fine for the small guy, but when one of the bigger chaps tried it he got down okay but then got stuck. Try as he might, wobbling all over the place, he couldn't get back up off the running boards. Then he started to get cramp as well! My friend, Bill Letts, was the other big guy and he watched helplessly as, in the end, his partner slowly wobbled to a standstill and fell off the scooter into the ditch! Bill didn't try this method of riding; what he'd seen was enough to put him off.

There was a running backwards problem with the Tina scooters, but this did not come to light until the small guy of the trio, proceeding up the Parade in Leamington Spa, was forced to stop quickly at some traffic lights that had changed against him. He stalled the scooter, but started it again with one quick prod of the kickstarter. What he didn't know, however, was that the engine, being a two-stroke and on fairly advanced ignition timing, was now running backwards! When the lights changed he whacked the throttle open for a quick getaway (you just opened the throttle to go and the centrifugal clutch came into play automatically), and whizzed backwards into the front of a double-decker bus waiting behind! I don't know who was the more surprised, the little guy or the bus driver.

The Tina had a start and drive switch mounted just below the handlebars on the front frame panel. The idea was that you switched to the start position, which activated a governor, preventing the engine revving sufficiently to bring into play the automatic transmission. Once the engine had been kickstarted you could, when seated, switch to drive which removed the governor and by opening the throttle, away you went. It really was simple but some still got it wrong, resulting in accidents. Our worst nightmare of an accident occurred on a sunny, summer's morning during a press release photographic session. ET was in residence and, on the spur of the moment, decided to take a spin on the new scooter along the main drive between the front of the factory and the lawn, which was just wide enough for two normal-sized cars to pass. Four inch high kerbstones acted as edging, preventing anyone from driving or riding off the tarmac surface and on to the lawn.

Word filtered down that ET was about to emerge from his eyrie, so three of us service chaps decided to wander around to the front and watch the proceedings: after all, this was going to be a momentous occasion as none of us had ever seen ET ride a motorcycle, let alone a scooter. I know he took part in the Gaffer's Gallop with my old service manager, A St J Masters, and Bob Fearon, then works manager, to publicize the Terrier launch — but this was different. As we wandered up the drive and around the end of the new experimental department building, we joked amongst ourselves about the unlikely event of the great man and the scooter parting company! With raucous laughter, we fantasized over the imaginary event,

A Tina, resplendent in full touring kit.

adding our own outlandish ideas as to how it would happen, with each successive idea becoming more and more bizarre.

Standing well to one side, we waited until ET finally appeared and, with a trio of publicity men, was ushered to the innocent-looking, lavender-coloured machine. A number of shots with him sitting smilingly on the thing were soon accomplished by the photographers and the dreaded moment arrived for the scooter to be started up. One of the publicity chaps approached ET and attempted to show him the correct starting sequence. We heard him say "This is how you start it and this is what you do to drive off, Sir." "Yes, yes, I know how it works" came ET's swift and irritable reply as he pulled on the fuel tap and took a quick stab at the kickstart pedal. We can only surmise that he didn't put the dreaded switch into the start position first and, being an old motorcyclist, gave the little beast a fistful of throttle, too! This small, Saville Row-suited

Tales of Triumph & Meriden

figure seated on what was now a lavender-coloured rocket, shot across the drive and, at a shallow angle, made contact with the kerb. The small-diameter front wheel, deflected by the sudden contact with the obstacle, flicked the scooter to one side and off ET shot. Luckily, at the angle and speed that things happened, he was pitched unceremoniously on to the grass rather than the tarmac.

For a split second, none of us could believe our eyes — the impossible had happened. My friend, Stan Truslove, had just taken a long drag on his cigarette as the mishap occurred and, in a desperate attempt not to laugh out loud, was turning purple with suppressed laughter and tobacco smoke. With eyes bulging, he stared at me helplessly, not daring to make a noise. Not a sound was heard, no one was prepared to chance a laugh, a light-

A close-up of the automatic transmission of the Tina.

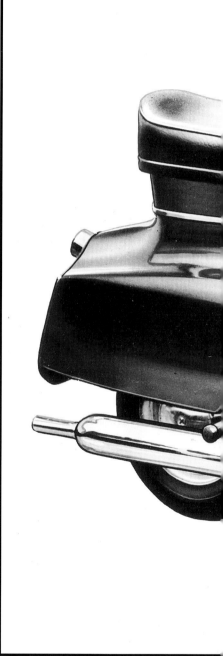

The T10 scooter - a modified Tina - a more refined animal than its predecessor, with the majority of problems cured.

hearted remark, a whimper, a smirk, nothing; it was more than our jobs were worth. We edged as nonchalantly as possible around the corner of the experimental department to be out of sight of the dreadful scene before any of us dared even titter! Stan at last exhaled his smoke and his face was returning to a more normal colour as we started laughing and talking excitedly on our walk back to the office. Once inside, we sat at our respective desks and, as if a signal had been given, burst into long, uncontrollable laughter. I don't think ET ever rode a scooter again after that episode.

The natural progression from the Tina was the slightly redesigned T10, with the notorious switch now incorporated in the seat and activated by body weight. It was reasoned by our designers that you couldn't engage the drive unless you were sitting on the beast - wrong - and I witnessed a classic example of this mistaken belief in the finishing shop some time later. One of the chaps was checking a T10 with the machine on its centre stand and holding the throttle open to check that the governor was operating, thus preventing the drive from engaging. A colleague, leaning forward over the scooter to speak, placed one hand on the seat and, whoosh, off went the T10, careering into a couple of bikes and knocking them flying.

One of the friends that I still come into contact with, Mr Jim Lee, an ex-tester who now runs his own export and shipping business, remembers well another failing of the automatic scooter — belt inversion. This particular problem manifested itself when the unit and automatic drive was revved beyond its limits. A typical example, related by Jim, took place on a beautiful day during a test run down the old A429 to Cirencester. Riding a 98cc on mileage wasn't exactly awe-inspiring, which is where the stooping down on the running board came in, which at least livened up droning along at 40 to 45mph! Cresting the brow of a hill, Jim decided to stoop to get more speed and, soon, on flat-out throttle, he topped a dizzying 50mph. All of a sudden the rear wheels locked solid. Luckily, Jim was able to regain his seat and control the scooter until at about 25mph he and the machine parted company. After 'phoning the factory from a call-box and getting a lift back with the dented scooter in the works Thunderbird combo, it was found that when the automatic transmission pulley closed up, thus forcing the drive-belt outwards to increase the gearing, the belt, when attaining the maximum position, flipped over and inverted itself, locking up the drive. Another major re-think was needed!

An unusual twin Tina prototype - put together by Willie and others - appeared from out of the experimental department. Basically, it was two scooters side-by-side which were joined by a large centre section, thereby making it a four-wheeler. The two engines were retained and were controlled by double throttle cables from one twistgrip, and a tie-bar joined the two front wheels so that only one pair of handlebars was required. These remained on the right-hand scooter, so that the left-hand one was on the same side as a sidecar would be. It was a very lively thing which was used around the factory roads for many and varied purposes, but mainly as Willie's personal transport! If you happened to be walking along the back drive alongside the repair shop when you heard this thing approaching (it sounded like demented bumble bees in a jam jar), you got out of the way quick or risked being chased by the demonic Willie. It never went into production, though, and, as far as I can remember, was sold off when the factory closed. A pity!

The testers were all a good bunch of chaps and, even now after 30 years, we all meet up once a year to keep in touch and keep our memories alive.

Repair Shop again!

After a few more months on test I transferred to the rectification (knacker gang) for a while, then, just in time for the introduction of the new unit construction 650s, moved back up to the repair department. By this time a few changes had occurred; people had left and new faces replaced them. Les Williams had gone to the experimental department where he and Percy were to attain fame in later years with the racing three cylinder bike s.

Working practices had also altered drastically during the period I had been away from the old place. For one thing the unions - the Birmingham Sheet Metal Workers Union, the Transport and General Workers Union, the AUEW and a few more I can't remember - had started to flex their muscles and bring in restrictive practices. When I started at Meriden with Bozzy and Reg Hawkins, if we had a bike with a small scratch on the paintwork we could quite easily and quickly apply some paint and then cut it back and polish it - job done! But not any more. Now the part had to be taken off and sent into the paint shop for the required work. This approach applied to all aspects other than pure fitting, such as knocking the odd dent out of a metal part but not, on the whole, to work under warranty on new bikes because if there was a problem with a part it was renewed and not repaired. But when the display team bikes came back at the end of each season for rework, whereas before a fitter could totally strip out the bike and carry out any repairs himself, including tin-bashing, touching-up paintwork or even truing a wheel or two, this was now taboo. Items had to be taken to the appropriate part of the factory for attention and you couldn't take it yourself; that had to be done by the material handlers, as they were called. If the material handler who operated in your area or workshop was busy it was tough: it waited. Jobs now took longer to do and obviously the cost went up pro rata. Somehow the camaraderie had gone from the shop, apart from a few close friends the fitters were mostly new young chaps, strangers who came from all walks of life.

In late 1961 and early 1962 we had problems with the Metropolitan Police

6T machines in Charcoal Grey, supplied some time in 1960 and 1961. They were down on power with poor, slow running, and suffered various other complaints which included poor handling, necessitating a frame change (to the new duplex frame with the slightly altered head angle for 1962). The motors were stripped and - to give more power - the camshafts changed from the original E4220 Dowson to the Tiger 110 type. The carburettors were also rejetted to suit the new cams. There were a host of other things that we did and, although I can't remember exactly what, I do recall that the registration numbers began LAH and a lorry delivered eleven bikes a week to the repair shop, taking eleven completed ones back on its return journey.

Each of the bikes had to be performance tested and Percy was the man for that! I was one of the chaps who met Cannonball, the works lorry driver who took eleven bikes to MIRA on the appointed day. After we had checked the bikes, Percy would take each one through the timing lights on the strip and its speed would be recorded to three decimal places. The slowest of these reworked 6Ts was put through at 111mph! Pretty quick, eh? All-in-all we did about 200 of these bikes and, as far as I'm aware, having talked to the big London coppers who rode them, they were satisfied with the work.

The Dowson camshaft, part number E4220, wasn't exactly a success until many years later, when it was discovered, almost by accident, that it was excellent for racing engines. Originally designed by Jack Dowson, a young chap in the drawing office, to replace the E3275 ramp cam used mainly in the Speed Twin, Thunderbird and some later Tiger 100 models, it was fitted to the 1960 to 1961 6T duplex-framed Thunderbird. As a result, the service repair shop was inundated with complaints concerning poor tickover and erratic slow running, which no amount of alteration to ignition timing and carburation could rectify. After a meeting at the factory with the people concerned, the various managers agreed that the E4220 cam would no longer be fitted to the 6T Thunderbird and would be replaced by the E3325 Tiger 110 camshaft, as fitted by the service department repair shop to the Metropolitan Police 6T machines. In fact, all 6T pre-unit duplex-framed Thunderbirds built between engine numbers D7727 and D11192 were equipped with the Tiger 110 cams and, as such, had no wheel mark stamped next to the engine number as did the previous models. This meant that the inlet camshaft pinion had to be meshed with the dash mark on the intermediate wheel and, at the same time, the tappet clearances amended from 0.010 inch clearance all round for the E4220 to 0.002 inch on the inlets and 0.004 inch on the exhaust for the E3325 form cam. To complement the camshafts, an alteration to TR6 Trophy specification was made for the ignition timing and carburettor. The 6T Thunderbird really did perform well after this modification, but the price paid was an increase in engine rattle and overhead clatter as the T110 cams didn't have quietening ramps!

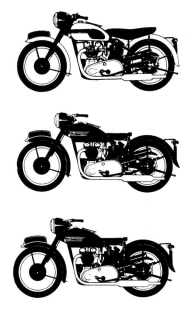

Another small electrical problem that arose on the duplex-framed magneto-powered models - the Tiger 110, Trophy TR6 and Bonneville T120 - was one of overcharging. If the machines were ridden fast for any distance in daylight, the generator put too much charge into the battery. To reduce the output when the lights were in the off position, we fitted an extra wire, coloured green/white, from the number 7 terminal on the light switch to the green/white connection on the rectifier. This remedy only worked with overcharging when the light switch was in the off position, and if overcharging persisted with the headlights on, a higher wattage main bulb was fitted to compensate.

Repair Shop again!

Generally, the magneto/AC lighting bikes of 1960 to 1962 were very good and much liked by both riders and the chaps who worked on them under warranty.

We were fast approaching the advent of the new 650cc units but just how we were going to manage them in the workshop (to work on, I mean), we didn't know. It was easy to remove the pre-unit motors by dismantling the transmission completely, unbolting the motor and lifting it out of the frame, but this new thing would require the muscles of Goliath! Chaps were worried they'd give themselves a hernia after the first job and a mobile hoist was considered, but that was really impracticable, so we opted to give each other a hand when and if required. It took us a while, but things worked out okay in the end.

We had a new foreman now in Bert Carter, and my old friend, Reg Hawkins, became the charge-hand. The Police were after a new model and the good old 6T Thunderbird was revamped in its unit construction form. I was given the job of building the first motorway white 6TP and was asked by Mr Nelson, the service manager, to ride it down to Scotland Yard to show them. I left it there and came back on the train and from that first one came hundreds of orders for more.

Sid Shilton on a 1960 T120 at the Meriden main gate.

One of my old testing friends, Norris Harrison, had moved on to police liaison with Mr Neale 'Sid' Shilton, who later wrote a super book all about the Triumph at Meriden. He was also called 'Mr Triumph' and enjoyed the distinction of coming up with the acronym (Stop Anything In No Time). From then on, all Police bikes were officially called the Saint. He must have ridden hundreds of thousands of miles all over the world, demonstrating the bike and its capabilities in order to secure sales.

The workshop went along quite well, turning out repaired bikes on the day appointment system and overhauling components for the service exchange schemes. We had a new manager in the form of John R Nelson, a graduate of Cambridge and, in everyone's eyes, a damn good bloke. There was, inevitably, more happening in the States so John was off across that side of the Pond more often than not. In his place, a friend of mine for years to come, the incredible Alex Scobie, took over as assistant service manager. More about him later ...

One morning, whilst we were all working on day appointments or whatever, a strange apparition appeared at the bottom of the repair shop just inside the rubber swing doors and next to our service exchange stores. The figure

Alex Scobie - Road Tester Extraordinaire and Man of Iron - in 1959.

Tales of Triumph & Meriden

177 EUE - the original Police 6T with full kit. This bike was maintained by Mike Crowther and the author and travelled many thousands of miles demonstrating the prowess of the 'Saint.' Note the modified external spring forks and sports front mudguard.

stood there for some minutes without moving, while gradually more and more chaps in the shop started to take notice. Its clothes were weird to say the least. It was dressed in an old, long, brown canvas riding coat which nearly reached the floor and was tied around the waist with hairy string. From under the edge of the coat peeped the largest pair of Wellington boots I'd ever seen — they must have been size twelve or fourteen. The 'thing' wore an old crash helmet that almost came down over its eyes and, with the collar of the coat turned up, you could barely make out anything of its face. Both arms were dug down deep into the capacious pockets of the coat. By now, just about everyone in the repair shop was looking, including Bert Carter and Reg Hawkins. It was strange, really, as neither of them made any move towards it to see what it wanted. We started work on our jobs again, but kept on watching with interest.

Suddenly the apparition began to shuffle to one side, getting ever nearer to the open side of a rack containing service exchange speedos. Our curiosity was up! Bert and Reg, both of them pipe smokers, had, with steely glints in their eyes, stoked up, puffing away in preparation for a sortie down to the workshop to see what the hell was going on. Then it happened: with the speed of a striking snake, the thing's left hand shot out, grabbed a speedo head and plunged it deep into its pocket! With utter disbelief on his face, Bert turned to Reg and said "Did you see that?" As one, jaws set in firm resolve, they started down the shop towards the thing. As quick as a flash, it turned and vanished through the swing doors. Bert and Reg were running now and followed it through the doors — but couldn't find it - it had disappeared into thin air. The works gateman-cum-policeman was called and made a thorough search of the area, but not a sign was found. Indeed, we wondered if we'd been seeing things until about fifteen minutes later Willie strolled into the bottom of the shop and, when we looked later on, the speedo head was back where it should be, on the shelf! For many days to come, whenever Willie passed through the repair shop on his way to either the stores or the main factory, he always had a grin on his face. In subsequent casual conversations, several of us tried to pump him about the strange thing we had seen but he always maintained he knew nothing about it and I almost believed him, but not quite ...

Some of the least troublesome machines to come into the repair shop were the C range models, the 350cc Twenty One (or 3TA as it was later called) and the 490cc Speed Twin or 5TA. Running on standard 6 volt AC coil ignition, they were quiet, smooth and economical. Not so the energy transfer ignition T100A which had higher compression ratios and E3134 camform camshafts! The model started out okay but, as miles were covered and things loosened up (especially in the distributor), starting problems and misfiring occurred.

With energy transfer ignition, timing has to be exactly right; not to within one or two degrees but exact, otherwise trouble arose. Therefore, a decision was made to return all the T100A machines that came back into the repair shop to the ordinary AC coil ignition specification. Generally, all Tiger 100A models, after engine number H22430, were changed to coil, which made them a nice, easy-starting little sportster, easily topping 95mph under favourable conditions. The energy transfer system was also used on the Tiger Cub model T20SL which then became prone to starting and running problems after wear occurred in the automatic advance and retard mechanism inside the Lucas distributor. Basically, the problem was due to wear in the auto unit bob-weight pivot pins, which allowed the cam to advance out of range. The ignition timing could be set so that the bike started easily on the kickstart but misfired at higher revs. If the timing was altered with the engine running to eliminate the misfire, once it stopped it was impossible to restart without resetting the ignition again!

Lucas came up with a speedy and relatively simple remedy, however: a steel sleeve with a 0.005 inch wall thickness which fitted over the automatic advance and retard stop peg inside the distributor, thus reducing the effective range of the auto and keeping it within usable limits. I think we were all re-

The author with the first white 'Saint'. Leaning on the bike is F S 'Stan' Truslove, a good friend, sadly, no longer alive.

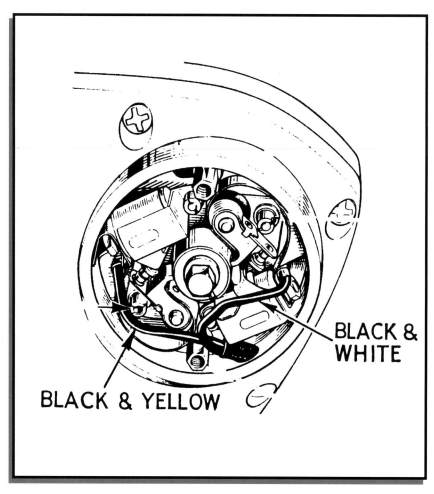

BLACK & WHITE

BLACK & YELLOW

The first Lucas contact breaker, designated 4CA.

lieved when the energy transfer was discontinued and the Cub sports models went to AC lighting and ignition systems. At least the kickstart didn't bite your leg and rattle your teeth when attempting to start up!

The next electrically-promoted problem which caused a great many people to scratch their heads occurred on the 350cc unit construction Tiger 90 and manifested itself in the form of a tightening up or seizing. After riding a few miles, and when the engine was up to temperature, the bike would start to slow down. Opening the throttle more would merely make matters worse, causing the engine a make a loud knocking noise and labour hard, almost as if the rear brake was being progressively applied. It was some time before the fault could be pinpointed by the Lucas backroom boys, but eventually it was and it turned out to be nothing more sinister than a wrongly ground auto advance cam in the 4CA twin contact breaker assembly. The actual grinding of the cam was fine except for the drop-off at the back of the camform, which was too severe and caused a random spark when the points closed. This random spark occurred somewhere near bottom dead centre and was the cause of pre-ignition.

A simple, over-the-phone action was worked out by the service department to ascertain whether the machine being talked about was suffering with what had by now been dubbed 'Tiger Ninety-itis.'

If a customer or dealer rang, claiming a bike was seizing under load, we simply instructed him to ride the bike until the fault occurred, then quickly stop, lift the seat and remove the centre Lucas connector from the rectifier. If the sluggish, pre-ignition or seizure symptoms disappeared and the engine note and performance once again became crisp, this indicated that the auto advance unit should be changed from the original fitted (part number 54415750) to the new reprofiled 160 degree unit (part number 54041118). From engine number H51616, all C range 350cc and 500cc units were fitted with the redesigned unit and service bulletin number 276 detailed the operation so that dealers could attend to units that had escaped the net and might appear later on outside their particular warranty period.

Once the energy transfer and 'Tiger Ninety-itis' problems were sorted, most of the jobs that came into the repair shop were more run-of-the-mill. One such problem that the dealers couldn't stop, though, was cylinder base oil leaks on all the C range models. The 3TA, T90, T100A, 5TA and T100SS all at one time or another had this particular oil leak which could not be cured by removing the top of the motor down to the cylinder base joint and carefully rebuilding and remaking the joints and seals with fresh gaskets. Everyone thought that the leak emanated from the bottom pushrod tube seal as the oil was always first to appear around both the inlet and exhaust tappet blocks. It was sometime before an inquisitive fitter, having built an engine once for the problem, had the job rejected by the tester because oil had started to seep out again around the bottom of the pushrod tube area. Upon dismantling the second time, he concentrated on the cylinder base studs threaded into the crankcase and found that, out of the eight studs, four of them immediately either side of both inlet and exhaust tappet blocks were not into blind holes but into open holes straight through into the crankcase immediately above both camshafts. When these four particular studs were removed and examined, oil was found on the threads. Under running conditions with the engine hot, crankcase compression was forcing oil up the threads, then up through the stud hole in the cylinder barrel flange. After a while, it would find its way out from underneath the base nut itself, appearing either side and around the bottom of the tappet block and pushrod tube.

Once the cause was found, the remedy was simply to remove the barrel and, after unscrewing the four offending studs and cleaning them, coat their 3/8 inch BSF threads in jointing compound, finally screwing them back into the crankcase and locking them home hard. I find this remedy still works when I get either a 350 or 500cc engine unit with cylinder base oil leaks that have confounded all previous attempts at a cure.

The 1964 season saw the introduction of what was later to become designated the French Army Cub, which was a sports T20M based on the International Six Days Trial models prepared by the competition department for the British Army team riders. The modifications to the Cub were commonsensical and, as such, appealed to not only the Ministry of Defence, but to the French Army as well who wanted 7000 examples of this model to be used by its soldiers, mainly in Algeria and the North African deserts. The number ordered was originally 7000 machines, but this order was never fulfilled due to events that I shall explain.

Our Tiger Cub wizard, Benny Marshall, reworked a bike to the standards required by AID (Admiralty Inspection Directorate), with a government inspector present. This meant heavier than standard rear wheel and gearbox sprockets with rear chain to suit, altered or repositioned drain and access points for oil changes and heavier control cables. The centre-stand had to be reinforced, as did the rider/s footrests, along with a host of other minor modifications which included cable routing and wiring loom repositioning.

It was upon this lovely little machine that the French Army Cub was finally based. Monsieur Guy Peron, owner of CGCIM, Triumph's French distributor in Paris, and the person with whom all liaison between the factory and the French Army took place, was finally delighted with it.

The first batch of 200 machines was sent over from Meriden. Finished in drab matt olive green livery, they actually looked quite good, but then things went drastically wrong because, on the decision of the BSA board who now governed us at Meriden, Cub production was moved to Armoury Road, Birmingham. Whether or not it was down to the inevitable problems that occur when total production of such a complex item as a complete motorcycle —

plus all the manufacturing and machining operations of its component parts — is moved lock, stock and barrel ten miles up the road, I don't know, but we were in deep trouble. Monsieur Peron was not happy, nor were the spokesmen for the French Army, as the agreements had been made with Meriden where the Cub had been manufactured since its birth and not with BSA. Not only was the second batch of Birmingham-built machines delivered to France behind schedule, but the bikes suffered build quality problems. Chaps on the production line, used to their own make of machine, were not aware of the very particular ways in which this or that part was fitted, as agreed at the outset with CGCIM and the French Army. When this first batch of BSA Cubs arrived in Paris and was uncrated, the telephone lines almost burst into flame with the complaints. It was decided to send Benny Marshall and Stan Truslove over there in an attempt to sort out what was wrong and decide on a plan of action to remedy the situation. Both were well versed on the Cub, so it was agreed they should be put up in a hotel and stay in France for as long as it took to sort things out to the satisfaction of our French customers; they were in Paris for six weeks!

Many years later, when speaking to Benny about the fiasco, he remembered the French Army Captain with whom he liaised during this time. Conversation was in German, because Benny couldn't speak French and Stan only had a smattering, but because Benny had been a prisoner of the Germans during the war, he was fluent in that langauge as, fortunately was the French Army Captain. Poor old Stan had to stand by and let the two rattle on in a language he didn't understand, which didn't please him at all as he was supposed to be in charge of the operation.

One of the main faults was with the centre stand. Instead of the special reinforced heavy-duty item, complete with cutaway to miss the silencer, as agreed, the standard part had been painted matt green and fitted. Of course, they had to be changed but, first of all, the correct ones had to be delivered to Paris quickly, very quickly. The demand was passed on to BSA and we were assured that the correct stands, duly painted in the correct colour, were, even as we spoke, being loaded aboard an aircraft at Birmingham airport bound for Paris, Orly. For two long days, and after innumerable telephone calls between Paris and Meriden, CGCIM and Orly in an effort to find out where the centre stands were, they were at last located - in Canada! An irate telephone call from our Canadian importer, demanding to know why he had been sent a crate containing Tiger Cub parts in olive drab when he had ordered no such items, did not go down too well with us at Meriden. Full of embarrassment, we had to contact CGCIM and try to explain.

This one episode serves to illustrate the degree of trouble we were facing and, indeed, later on, when spare frames were required, a consignment of freshly painted matt green Bantam frames were only just waylaid in time to prevent them being shipped to France! We realized that the BSA people had run out of T20 Cub frames, and had no intention of making any more at any cost. The French could have Bantam frames or nothing at all!

At this point, we at Meriden felt not only betrayed by our colleagues at Birmingham, but also an accute sense of dismay because we knew now that the Cub tooling had all been destroyed and we would never see the little Triumph built again. I don't think the French contract was ever completed. Pity, because it was a good little bike, really. I built one myself out of bits left over in 1966 and still ride it today. With only 15,000 genuine miles on the clock, it pulls along at a good 70 miles per hour and returns 90 miles to the gallon.

The BSA attitude was further highlighted by another erstwhile unexplained occurrence whilst Benny was in Paris on the Cub job. Monsieur Peron had customers for six Bonnevilles which he ordered and requested during the Paris Motorcycle Show in October 1968. After a few weeks, two Bonnevilles arrived. "But where are the remaining four?" Monsieur Peron asked. Eventually they arrived but accompanied by a number of unordered BSA machines. By now, all the Triumph sales people had been replaced by BSA personnel based in a Portakabin on the front drive at Meriden. Their directives were clear: push the BSA models at all costs. But CGCIM in Paris didn't want BSA bikes, they wanted Triumph. Despite repeated calls to the sales department nothing happened with regard to the removal of the unwanted BSA machines, and it wasn't until May 1969 that Monsieur Peron told the sales department in no uncertain terms that unless the machines were removed forthwith, a storage charge would be levied against the BSA group. Within days, a German lorry arrived and the unwanted BSAs were taken to a German dealer - desperate times indeed ...

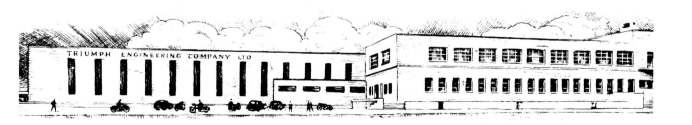

(Bad) vibrations

By this time we were experiencing vibration problems, resulting in the 650 machines cracking brackets, mudguards and petrol tanks. This was vicious, high frequency stuff that we couldn't seem to cure by altering the balance factors. It wasn't unusual to have a new bike of only three months usage come into the repair shop, accompanied by its owner to talk to and show the management the problems. One such chap emptied his riding suit pockets of literally dozens of light bulbs he had fitted as the filaments inside kept being vibrated off. One of the bikes I worked on had a split along the length of the rear mudguard, straight down the centre. When I removed the rear number plate and the mudguard mounting bolts, it came off in two halves!

Our only option was to put our trust in the experimental boys and hope that they could tone down this high frequency stuff to a more acceptable level. After all, road speeds were increasing all the while and the Triumph twin engine, as old as it was, had to live in this environment. Most of all the 650cc problems coming in now were to do with vibration and, at one point, we even ran out of the F7004 petrol tank which was the four-gallon, home-market item fitted to the TR6 and T120. This tank had the single mounting ear at the back and, as a regular as clockwork, off it would come. The stupid thing about it was that you knew the part you were fitting as a replacement under warranty was going to go in just the same way within a few weeks. All we could do was take out the engines, strip the cranks, rebuild them and be ultra-ultra careful in the balancing to get them smack on at an 87 per cent balance factor. The crank had to remain stationary on the knife-edges in any one of the eight positions required. This would at least rule out the crank in any further work should it be necessary. We also ensured that all the nuts, bolts and studs that held the motor and engine steadies could be pushed in by hand, and none of the holes were out of alignment. It's so often the case when you are trying to put an engine back into the frame that you find the last couple of studs half a hole out, and then the temptation to bang them in with a big hammer be-

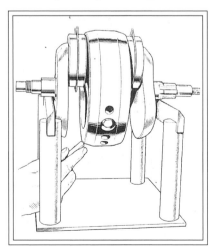

The simple but effective method of crankshaft balancing using the service repair shop 'knife-edges'.

A nightmare: the 650 Bonneville, which suffered from frame breakages, oil leaks, poor brakes and front mudguards falling off. Warranty costs rocketed.

comes too great. You do it, and end up with only threads on one half of the stud or bolt; you can't start the nut and you've forced the thing into the hole, causing stress.

We were always told to take our time and make sure to push all the studs or bolts through with our fingers (you may even have to jiggle the motor about in the frame a bit). If you can't push a bolt through, open the offending hole out a little with a round file until you can; then and only then, start to tighten everything. I've seen so many chaps fit unit motors, put the back engine plates on, but before putting the nuts and bolts through they've tightened the front and bottom through studs, which makes life very difficult. We also tried rubber-mounting exhaust systems, but that wasn't at all popular, because you had to leave the joint at the cylinder head loose, otherwise it would crack the cups off the pipe. Not very good, so we reverted to the normal fitting.

Tales of Triumph & Meriden

One of the biggest contributing factors to bad vibration was incorrect ignition timing. The Lucas 4CA contact breaker assembly was a fiddly thing to set up properly with a stroboscope, mainly because you could only time one cylinder by moving the back plate on its elongated adjuster holes. Once that cylinder was set correctly and you put the strobe on to the other side and found that that was a few degrees out, you couldn't alter the second one to correct it otherwise you would end up upsetting the first one. The only way to set the second cylinder, after the first one had been set at the correct degrees of advance at between 1800 and 2000rpm, was to adjust the actual gap on the contact points. It usually equated to 0.001 inch equalling two degrees, so by opening the points gap by an extra 0.002 inch you increased the degrees of advance by four. Conversely, by closing down the point gap you retarded the degrees of advance. Although this method was effective, you had to be pretty exact in your work and, obviously, to be spot on you had to have the kit to do it, and not every bloke who bought a 650 twin had this sort of equipment hanging up in his garage.

After a while, the Joseph Lucas engineers came up with the reliable 6CA contact breaker assembly, with independently adjustable points. This allowed you to adjust one cylinder dead on, then start on the other set of points without messing up the first side. When you consider we were working to within a single degree, it was pretty exacting stuff. After the motor had been assembled with a nicely balanced flywheel at the new balance factor, the ignition timing set correctly and both carburettors set and balanced, things weren't too bad!

Later, in 1970 when I was on the service staff, I did actually have a meeting with the UK sales director with a view to replacing under warranty a complete bike for one chap who had been back to the factory so many times with his new 1970 T120 and lost countless days off work keeping his day appointments. We just couldn't seem to get this thing right; it really buzzed with a bad HF (high frequency) vibration. Alex Scobie, who was the assistant service manager, took it out on test to confirm the service department tester's findings and, upon his return, told me to go ahead with my request. I did get a new replacement bike for the Oxfordshire gentleman which, in the end, he was very pleased with, together with Triumph service.

During 1966/7 the vibration problems continued unabated. We coped as best we could but, once again, it was pretty demoralising to think that the majority of bikes coming off the track and going to home market dealers were, sooner or later, going to find their way back to Meriden for free-of-charge work under warranty for that damned vibration problem.

One chap who didn't seem bothered by it was Steve McQueen, the motorcycling film star. He was actually a very good rider, so much so he became a member of the American Vase B team for the International Six Day Trials held in some Eastern Eu-

The new 6CA unit, with independently adjustable contact points, making ignition timing setting much easier.

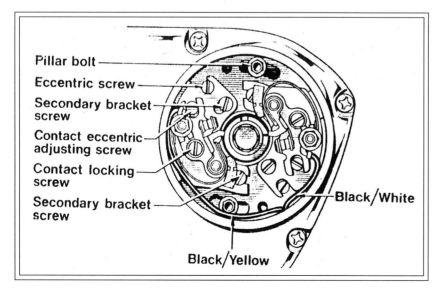

Pillar bolt
Eccentric screw
Secondary bracket screw
Contact eccentric adjusting screw
Contact locking screw
Secondary bracket screw
Black/White
Black/Yellow

ropean country (where, I can't remember now). Quite a charismatic character, you could feel McQueen's magnetism when he was near you. He was intense in most of the things he did and didn't mind taking chances on the Triumphs he rode; witness this in films like *On any Sunday* and *The Great Escape*. I had the pleasure of working on his 650 TR6 and, whilst it was up on the workbench I discovered, jammed underneath the petrol tank, a pair of his short-wristed chamois leather riding gloves. I offered them back to him and, guess what he said? "You keep 'em!" I didn't want to appear grabby so, as

Steve McQueen, motorcycle mad and a member of the American International Six Days Team. He was a very good rider.

Tales of Triumph & Meriden

Steve McQueen and the rest of the American ISDT. Sid Shilton is second from the right.

graciously as I could I said "Well I shouldn't, but thanks very much!"

He had done very well in the ISDT but come such an almighty cropper at one stage he'd actually flattened one exhaust pipe to the extent that the engine wouldn't run properly. Using his noddle, he spied an old forester chap chopping up wood with a long-handled axe, which McQueen used to chop shark gill slots into the offending pipe as gas outlets. Although noisy, the bike at least ran!

When he came to the factory, I was surprised at how small he was (this didn't seem to bother the office girls, though!) The day after he had gone someone mentioned the gloves I had and I began receiving propositions: you wouldn't believe the things I was offered for those gloves. I made up my mind not to part with them, however, and used them myself on fine days only, to preserve them as for long as I could. For a long while they were kept with my old riding coat hanging in the garage until my good lady wife decided to have a clear-out. She insists she asked me whether she could get rid of "that old coat hanging on the nail in the garage"; I guess she mentioned it at a time when I wasn't paying attention. Months later, I had been in the garage for some time before it dawned on me that the coat was gone and so too, unfortunately, had the gloves. It was with great sorrow that I read of Steve McQueen's death from cancer in later years. I shall always remember him - and those gloves.

Another famous film star to use Triumph motorcycles was the lanky, laconic Clint Eastwood. Although not such an avid motorcyclist as Steve McQueen, he did ride now and then, especially in some of the films he made, such as *Coogan's Bluff*, in which he played a lawman sent out to the big city to collect a prisoner and take him back to stand trial. Ultimately, the prisoner escapes and there follows a frantic motorcycle chase in which Eastwood rides a Triumph Trophy TR6 and the escapee a T100C. Eastwood does actually ride but experienced motorcyclists will detect that certain parts of the chase are speeded up, which does detract from the film somewhat.

One of the most glaring examples of Hollywood continuity foul-up occurs in another Eastwood film called *Magnum Force*. At the end of the film he and David Soul are chasing each other on Moto Guzzi Californians, equipped for highway patrol work, across the flight deck of a mothballed aircraft carrier anchored in San Francisco bay. As David Soul rides off the end of the flight

Clint Eastwood with co-star, Tisha Sterling, during the making, in 1968, of Coogan's Bluff. Clint chases the 'baddie' (who's riding a 500cc Tiger) on a TR6 through Central Park.

deck and into the sea, his Moto Guzzi changes in mid-air to a Triumph 650! I suppose that, at the time of making the film, it was more cost-effective to dump an old Triumph into the bay than a Moto Guzzi that in all probability had replaced the older Triumphs in real life service.

Getting back to vibration problems, we found that exact ignition timing helped towards eliminating this condition, so, to enable dealerships to set the new 6CA Lucas contact breaker assemblies accurately, a new stroboscope kit under part number CP207 was introduced around mid-1965. This measure took a lot of pressure off the service repair shop who, up to that time, were the only people equipped with the Suntester stroboscopic timing light.

It was also about this time that the positive oil feed to the exhaust cam followers came into being, due to premature cam lobe wear after only short mileages.

As well as introducing positive cam oiling on the 650cc units in 1966, two years later the sump capacity (oil at any given time in the bottom of the crankcase during normal running) was increased to help and increase splash lubrication of camshafts, followers and lower cylinder walls. The vibration problems experienced on the larger unit 650s, funnily enough, didn't materialise on the smaller, higher revving 500cc units, which leads me to think that the problems with the larger twins were all to do with rigidity. The earlier pre-unit motors did vibrate but it was liveable with due to the bike's overall flexibility. Having separate engine, gearbox and transmission, a lot more give - and, indeed, forgiveness - was apparent, but, with the unit construction 650s and even the later 750 twins where the complete engine unit was a stressed member of a very rigid frame, there was no forgiveness at all. I can only think that, to completely eliminate vibration from unit Triumphs, one has to totally rubber-mount the engine in a way similar to that system used by Norton motorcycles of the era.

Work on twins under warranty for vibration faults carried on right up to the closure of Meriden in 1973 but the problems were never really overcome.

Fairy

We were frequently getting the Coventry, as well as Warwickshire, police riders coming in with their bikes to have problems attended to and it wasn't unusual to walk into the repair shop on any working day and find a large policeman in black riding gear sitting on the bench enjoying a mug of Arthur's tea while his bike was being worked on. One of the most regular visitors was a policeman of huge proportions called Mick Fairfield, nicknamed Fairy, who was at least 6 foot 5 inches tall and built like Stonehenge. He was the most likeable chap, except when he got mad.

Fairy's bike didn't perform too well, apparently, so he came into the repair shop to have it checked out after some lad on a 250cc Royal Enfield gave him a two-fingered salute and Fairy couldn't catch him! (Not surprising, really, considering Fairy's size, the 60 pounds of radio transceiver (transmitter/receiver) which wasn't transistorised then, plus all the kit carried in both panniers). I laughed when we emptied the rear panniers and watched the ever-growing pile on the floor: there was a bottle jack and handle (just in case he needed one, he said), a fire extinguisher (one of the old brass-bodied type), a full toolkit and lots of other bits of useless gear. We took off the pannier boxes and disconnected and removed the radio set-up (I forgot to mention that the bike was also fitted with a windscreen, crash bar and leg shields!) Once the bike had been divested of its police stuff, the tester took it for a run to determine whether performance was up to standard. It was obvious that all this extra equipment was going to make a difference, but also that it did have to be carried. What was decided then, broke with tradition, really: we were going to tune Fairy's bike to give him a bit more performance.

The camshafts were changed for Bonneville types and valve timing altered accordingly. The carburettor, as well as the rear wheel sprocket, were altered to lower the gearing and allow the motor to rev more easily. When it was all done Fairy was most impressed and went out looking for the lad on the 250 Enfield! It did cause problems with the other coppers, however, because now

Tales of Triumph & Meriden

PC Mike Fairfield aboard XWD 337 which was tuned to TR6 Trophy specification. Mick was six foot five of pure muscle and the 650cc engine had to work really hard to carry him!

they wanted their bikes doing as well. We carried out similar modifications on most of the local police bikes, because a lot of the bobbies were on the well-built side. These bikes were used on A and B roads as well as in towns, therefore, power from low down in the rev range was required with acceleration to boot!

Later on, when the Lancashire Constabulary went to Saints, they were built for life on the M6 motorway and consequently pulled higher gearing. The Lancashire County workshops were based at Preston and over the number of years that Triumphs were used, a lot of work and close liaison went on between Preston and Meriden. It was difficult trying to keep the bikes up to scratch, especially when two riders shared one bike, as it left little time during shift changeovers for maintenance. After speaking to ex-Lancashire motorway lads in later years, they admitted that apart from filling up with petrol and topping up the engine oil at the shift change, the poor old Triumphs got hammered.

Slowly, as Triumph's problems worsened, we lost more and more forces to BMW motorcycles, although the Saint was still selling in fairly large numbers abroad, thank goodness. The faults occurring on the police bikes were now more serious and it often meant taking a bench-tested engine to some police force's workshop and carrying out a quick, complete engine change. As the police workshops were well-equipped, and I carried my own toolkit in the back of the service department Cortina MkI Estate, Stan Truslove and I could change an engine unit in something less than 45 minutes. Soon we were travelling the length and breadth of the country, and changing complete engines in civilian bikes as well, due to the inherent faults that were dragging us down, especially with regard to warranty costs.

Fairy, and the rest of the policemen at Nuneaton in Warwickshire, decided to have an open night at their nick. All the service chaps were invited but not everyone could manage it, so only about ten of us turned up on the night at the Nuneaton police station. Fairy and Jim Meacham (another big motorcycling policeman), made us very welcome and, for a joke, I even had a taste of being locked in the cells for a while! They were good lads, though, and let me out in time for a superb supper where both the food and jokes were splendid. This was the end of our relationship with the North Warwickshire Constabulary Motorcycle Division. Although I cannot remember exactly when Fairy and his colleagues stopped calling into the repair shop, the place never did seem the same without them.

On the staff

I was being asked more and more to accompany our outside trouble-shooter on journeys to dealerships, mainly to swap an engine under warranty on a troublesome machine, or even work on a bike at a customer's home. I did many miles with Stan Truslove in the service department's Ford Cortina estate car.

Back in the workshop one morning, Dixie was working on a police bike that had problems inside the nacelle behind the headlight. As you can probably imagine, with the radio equipment, blue-flashing lights, charge boost switch and all the normal lighting and ignition wiring, it was packed pretty tight in there. I don't know what made me do it but, as I walked past the bike up the workshop (Dixie had his back to me), I blew a cloud of pipe smoke into the open nacelle! Dixie turned, saw the smoke billowing out of the inside of the headlight and nacelle and promptly panicked. Thinking the wiring had shorted and the whole lot was going up in smoke, he grabbed his pliers and snipped through the main battery feed wire! I'm afraid I didn't tell him then what I'd done as he probably wouldn't have appreciated it, but a few months later it came out in conversation and even after that sort of time-lapse I could see he wasn't impressed at all! Poor old Dixie, at least he only had to replace the one lead to the battery and no other damage was done.

It was approaching Christmas 1966 and I was invited to go and see Mr John Nelson in his office, where he offered me a job on the service office staff. He told me the conditions of the staff appointment, salary and what was expected. I would, of course, be expected to wear a dark suit, be clean-shaven and smart at all times as I would be coming into contact with customers. A desk with telephones, one internal (inter-departmental) and one GPO (Telecom), was supplied, plus a very nice easy chair with arms so that I could at least be comfortable. My location in the service office was facing John Nelson, next to the big office windows and adjacent to the door into reception. The duties were all-embracing, really, dealing with everything that was thrown

Tales of Triumph & Meriden

Chris Huber on his 850cc Moto Guzzi, the only non-Triumph machine to be rectified 'under warranty' in the service repair shop at Meriden.

my way, which included dictating replies to customer letters, whether they be enquiries or complaints, organizing the daily appointments, liaising with dealers, fixing up guarantee claims and helping the Metropolitan Police sort out recovered stolen vehicles at Chalk Farm, the headquarters of C10, the Stolen Vehicles Division of Scotland Yard.

Alex Scobie, dear old Alex, had one of the most beautiful speaking voices I had heard for many a long while and he taught me how to answer the telephone. He used to say "Never refer to yourself as Mister Hancox when someone asks to whom they are speaking — it's surname only!" During peak times I suppose the number of letters I dictated would be more than fifty a day. We used Philips dictaphones with cassette tapes and a small hand-held microphone. When you were really proficient, you could pick up a customer's letter and dictate on to tape an answer straight off the top of your head. If it was a letter of complaint, you did your best to get things sorted out without appearing patronising, and I usually extended an invitation to the customer to come along to the factory with his bike for a chat. Out of courtesy, I'd send a carbon-copy of the letter to his dealer so that he'd be in the picture. It's surprising the number of really unpleasant customers who, once they had been to the service department, turned into really nice guys; I can only assume that some of them had been messed about by their dealers and had come to the end of their patience. Once they saw that the factory cared, their whole attitude changed for the better.

The old service department tester, Stan Whitcombe (who, sadly, is no longer alive), had come in from the cold and was now a bench fitter. My old friend from production test, Bill Letts, came up to take his place. One of the funniest things that happened to me in the service department occurred one summer afternoon in 1971. It started with the reception bell ringing to let me know that a customer required attention. Finishing off a letter, I headed into reception to be faced by a tall, young, slim man dressed in a one-piece black leather riding suit. With him was a beautiful dark-haired young woman dressed in an identical manner. It appeared they were Swiss and, whilst touring England on their three-month-old bike, had experienced problems. Being near to the factory, they decided to call in and see if there was anything we could do.

Both Willie and I had been trying to learn German from Benny Marszalkowski who, as I wrote earlier, spoke the language fluently. With the smattering of knowledge I had, I discovered the chap's name was Chris Huber. With signs and the odd smile and nod of understanding I half sorted out that it was a gear selection problem. I thought at the time "That's funny, we're not getting any gear selection problems. Oh well, it must be a one off." I asked the couple to wait and explained that I'd go and fetch the tester (my friend Bill

Letts) who could, after a test run, give me a better idea of the problem. Walking back to the service reception with Bill, I explained their predicament and he said "Don't worry, I'll be as quick as I can and then we can do something to get 'em back on their way!" "Great," I thought. Introducing Bill, I left them to go out to the bike and returned to the office.

I had barely sat down when the door opened and Bill's head appeared round it. "We've got a problem. You'd better come and look" he said. I thought "Blimey, what's up now?" Heading outside, I opened the main door and stopped dead: the bike was a Moto Guzzi vee-twin! I was speechless, I just didn't know what to say, so went and fetched Benny out to have a word with the Swiss rider. It transpired that, coming up the old A5 from London, the gearchange was getting harder and harder and the clutch doing nothing much at all, until finally they turned on to the A45 where they found Meriden. We just couldn't see them stuck so the Guzzi went into the repair shop for examination. It was found that, in the bike's car-type clutch, a simple adjuster and its lock-nut had come loose and backed off, making the clutch almost inoperative. It was easy to readjust and lock things up again. We checked the gearbox oil level and Bill took it for a test run. Great, everything worked satisfactorily again. The Swiss pair loaded up, had another cup of tea and then off they went with lots of waves, but it was a long while before Bill and the repair shop boys let me forget that day ...

Life in the service department office continued at a hectic pace, with more and more directives flying about from on high about the problems being experienced. It was usually the service department, writing and distributing service bulletins, that saved the day but then, I would say that as I wrote quite a few of them!

Early in 1970, things had started to go wrong with the T150 Trident, which was devastating, especially as the fault was the breaking of the triplex primary chains which invariably scrapped the crankcase. This, of course, meant complete dismantling and rebuild with new parts under warranty. It was found that the cause of this chain breakage was the engine sprocket and the shock absorber being slightly out of alignment on assembly. The triplex chain, under load, had little sideways give and could not withstand the fearsome pounding meted out by the out-of-line sprockets, with dire consequences. It was a really big job to be covered under warranty, especially when coupled with oil pump pinion and centre piston failure. Things seemed to be stacking up ...

The Met

It was often the case that I received 'phone calls from a Sgt John Bright at C10, the stolen vehicles division of the Metropolitan Police at Scotland Yard and, over the years, we became good friends. Either he would come up to Meriden with information on stolen bikes, or I would catch a train at Coventry and go down to see him at Chalk Farm. It wasn't an enviable task, trying to sort out the parts that made up a stolen machine., and you had to be careful what you said in court as the defendant's lawyer could rip your evidence to shreds.

In the main, the majority of bikes stolen within the Greater London area were Triumphs. The thieves would, quick as a wink, load a bike into the back of a Transit van the first moment it was left unattended and take it to a lock-up garage where, in relative peace and quiet, it could be dismantled and the parts required stored away somewhere for future use; the remainder was sold off or dumped in the Essex marshes. On one of these occasions I went down to examine and verify bikes, parts of bikes and spares. John Bright had just concluded a successful prosecution based on metal filings hoovered up from some chap's carpet. These filings — from cutting up a bike frame — were forensically tied up to parts of a bike found dumped on a rubbish tip in the Docklands area. It really brought it home to me that you didn't stand much of a chance when the boffins got on to you!

Through meeting John and his mates, I later on enjoyed the company of Dave Minskip and the Police International Six Days Team. These were BIG blokes, all well over 6 feet 6 inches, who rode specially-prepared Police bikes in the ISDT. They were excellent Metropolitan Police riders, and certainly knew a thing or two. On one occasion four of them came up to Meriden in an unmarked Wolseley 6/90 for a meeting with my old friend Norris Harrison. He was liaising, obtaining the bikes, then passing them on for the required modification to enable them to be used in the International Six Days. I was invited along to The Bulls Head in Meriden for lunch, which was a most enjoyable meal with plenty of jokes thrown in! On arriving back at the factory we pulled up in the visitors car park, only to find that their Wolseley had been boxed in by a Mini-Clubman Estate. Norris said "Don't worry. I'll ask Pop Wright, the work's policeman, who it belongs to and get them to move it." "Don't bother" said Dave Minskip and with that he and his three mates grabbed a corner each and picked it up! They carried it about a car's length — just enough to get their own vehicle out — and then piled into their black Wolseley, waved so long and off they went! Norris and I just stood looking at each other in shocked silence: on the way back to the office Norris said "I shouldn't like to meet them in an alley on a dark night!"

I suppose I visited Chalk Farm quite a few times to sort out things, taking with me my engine and frame numbers lists and all the documentation that enabled me to determine what bit came from which bike. I never spoke to, nor heard of, John Bright after 1973.

Triple troubles

By now the Trident was enjoying outstanding sporting success, especially in America at Daytona where, rumour had it, it was the main reason for the Japanese bringing out their big multis. With people like Dick Mann and Gene Romero riding it, the Trident cleaned up, with nothing else getting anywhere near. Les Williams, Arthur Jakeman, Jack Shemens and Doug Hele had now got the thing flying, winning TT after TT The most famous of these bikes was, of course, Slippery Sam, named after Percy. Les still has the bike, but I think it is now on show at the National Motorcycle Museum for posterity.

In the service reception we were running further into trouble with transmissions on the three-cylinder machine flying apart, as well as the centre piston melting. The latter was mainly due to cylinder temperatures being too high (overheating) and the ignition timing had to be set very critically with a stroboscope to overcome this. I remember the publicity blurb put out by the factory after our bikes had retired from some race or other, having seized on the centre pistons and broken the conrods. Some wag was glibly notifying the motorcycling magazines that the work's bikes failed due to electrical faults which, in a way they did: the centre piston seized, causing the centre rod to break, which then punched its way out through the front of the crankcase and chopped through the HT leads of the ignition coils mounted at the front of the motor!

We didn't have production of the Triple at Meriden very long as BSA - by now suffering - wanted something to give its workforce to do, as it had with the Tiger Cub in 1967. There was also an awful 250cc machine called the Trophy, which was really a BSA Starfire. It was produced at Armoury Road and came off that production line together with its BSA counterpart. We had untold trouble with that thing: some brain-box decreed that, although the bike was to be built at Birmingham, all the warranty work and costs would be carried by Meriden. This, of course, left us wide open to all sorts of ungentlemanly deeds by the BSA workers, by now very resentful of Triumph. BSA hadn't been able to sell the Bantam two-stroke in the face of competition from the Cub, so the Cub was taken from Meriden to be built at Armoury Road to give the BSA blokes some work. They didn't, however, want to continue to build the Cub as it was, so it was made into a hybrid called the Bantam Cub, using Bantam cycle parts into which was grafted the Cub engine. Again, Triumph service had to carry the can for all repair work under warranty, and the frightening thing about this was that we at Meriden were only seeing the tip of the iceberg as there were thousands of little catastrophes out there waiting to happen. I couldn't help thinking of the bikes sent all over the world that had these inherent faults lying dormant, waiting to appear once the bikes were sold and put into commission. It was a sobering thought that popped into my mind with every guarantee claim that Frank Floydd, the claims assessor, handled. His pile of computer printouts for each week's claims was now so high on his desk you couldn't see him.

The 1969 Trident, timing side.

The first (and some say the best) of the 750cc Triples, the Trident in original form.

So, there it was; three Triumph models — the Cub, the 250 Trophy and

Tales of Triumph & Meriden

the Trident — built at Armoury Road but with all the after-sales work costs covered by Meriden. Not very satisfactory!

On occasion mistakes occurred at Meriden, due, mostly, to carelessness. One dealer rang me to say he was doing a pre-delivery test on a T100T Daytona he'd sold, but, after starting up, couldn't get any oil pressure or return to the tank. Upon removing the timing cover, he found to his amazement that there was no oil pump! If this was the case, he asked, how could the bike have been tested before despatch? I had to admit that I didn't know, but would certainly try to find out.

By now the road testers had been taken off the road and brought inside to run the bikes on newly installed rolling roads. These were booths with a pair of rollers set into the floor, and on the back wall a panel containing instruments and switches. There were clamps for the footrests and, by wheeling the bike into the booth and placing its rear tyre between the rollers, you could clamp it into position. After coupling up the instrumentation and petrol feed, putting oil in the tank, gearbox and so on, the bike could be started. On the rolling road it was possible to check electrics, oil, gears and brakes, but it was not the same as riding it and getting feedback through the seat of your pants! As I mentioned earlier, many of the old testers thought that the introduction of rolling roads was a major contributory factor in the drop in quality control.

The ill-fated Small Heath manufactured Triumph Trophy TR25W of 1969. Disliked by all at Meriden, it took huge chunks out of the warranty budget.

After all, the tester was the chap who said if the bike was fit for despatch and if he didn't get to ride it, how could he know?

I concluded that, with the finishing shop becoming evermore chaotic, a mix-up resulted in the Tiger 100T Daytona with no oil pump getting into the wrong queue and missing altogether the rolling road.

On the Daytona T100T models a large number of main-bearing failures were occurring after only a small mileage; as little as 180 or 200 miles, in some cases. This was blamed on faulty bearings supplied by the manufacturer. But, as we didn't know exactly when the faulty bearings had been supplied, or when they were first used, all we could do was wait for the complaints to start. Add to this the primary chain breakages on the Trident T150 and we were suddenly paying out mega-money on warranty work - again!

That sinking feeling

At the end of 1970, for the 1971 season, the Bauer frame was introduced. We considered the 1970 650 models to be pretty good in that area, so why mess about with another frame? Again, I suppose, it was down to a decision made by BSA and the group's design centre at Umberslade Hall (christened 'Mighty Marmalade Hall' or 'Slumberglade Hall' by the Triumph blokes!) Dr Bauer designed this awful oil-in-the-frame thing which, after it had gone into production, was found to be far too tall. One of the production and development chaps recalled that when the bike was off the stand and on its wheels, the rider couldn't touch the floor! I believe it was lowered by some 1.5 inches to improve matters. I still see Jim Lee, that very same tester, who said that you had to come to rest near the kerb as a chap of average inside leg measurement just couldn't reach the ground otherwise.

Alex Scobie returned from Umberslade after inspecting the new oil-in-the-frame 650 twin, full of indignation after being told to keep his mouth shut! Looking at the complete new bike (which, incidentally, was already in production), Alex had remarked that the frame saddle height was too high and should be lowered considerably. He had also pointed out the failures surrounding the design of the new conical twin leading-shoe front brake. Trying to make himself heard and point out these two main areas of forseeable problems (especially as he had previously ridden the bike and found the front brake faded like mad after one or two heavy stops), he was taken to one side and told to keep quiet as things were too far down the line to do anything about it.

One of the other problems with this frame was that it was impossible to remove the engine from the frame complete because of the large diameter oil bearing cross-bar, which caused untold headaches in the service repair shop, complicating procedures for both us and the dealers. However, the biggest warranty problem was yet to show itself ...

The frame was constructed of thin-walled tube which, I suppose, was alright except in the case of the sump housed at the bottom of the vertical saddle

Tales of Triumph & Meriden

Alex Scobie on JAC 769 in the pits at Montlhery. Allan Jeffries is filling the fuel tank (with Len Bayliss behind) and H G Tyrell-Smith topping up the engine oil. Other onlookers are FIM officials and spectators.

down-tube. On the bottom of this tube , below and to the rear of the gearbox, was the main sump plate which retained the complete oil capacity of the frame. Unfortunately, also fixed at this point were the centre stand pivot lugs. Suddenly we were receiving claims from UK dealers for frame changes, as well as day appointments for the same thing coming into the service repair shop. Then claims started arriving from abroad — America, Canada, Australasia, the Continent — boy, were we in trouble! This was the biggest single operation ever under warranty; it looked as if every bike that had gone out had to have the frame changed. The situation was worse in the US as the Americans, for some reason, would leave the bike on its stand, get aboard and attempt to kickstart the bike which, of course, caused stress on the stand pivot lugs and fractured the frame bottom (the oil sump, in effect) to which the stand pivot lugs were affixed. It was obviously no good attempting a repair, for the customer would understandably demand a new frame on his new bike. We were inundated with requests for day appointments into the workshop and, at one point, claims for frame changes were stacked up for over a month. It was a mess; suddenly, it wasn't a nice place to work anymore ...

The only light relief came in the form of either the Motorcycle Show at Olympia and Earls Court, or going out in the evening with my old friend, Alex Scobie, to give talks to various sections of the Triumph Owners Club, which would occur at varying intervals, usually on a Friday evening. If we had to go somewhere like Bedford, we'd finish an hour earlier than usual and go home to get ready. I'd meet Alex later, at his place in Allesley, and we'd go off in his car (for which he could claim expenses and fuel allowance) to wherever the talk was to be held.

It was one of my real delights to listen to Alex recount his Grand Prix testing days using the old A45, or his epoch-making stints on the 1949 Thunderbird at Montlhery in France. As I said earlier, he had the most beautiful speaking voice; he actually did all the announcing at Earls Court and later at the NEC motorcycle shows. We'd usually talk for about three-quarters of an hour each, him on his experiences, me on service procedures, and then throw the meeting open to questions. It used to be good fun, with plenty of laughs from both us two and the audience.

By now John Nelson had left to go to Norton Villiers, with Alex taking up the reins as manager. Although he was extremely able, I could see that we were getting even deeper into trouble with both the product and the unions, which were now so strong they virtually stopped production every day for some reason or another. I experienced their extreme inflexibility at first hand one day whilst in the service office. I had dictated a number of letters in reply to customers' queries and complaints, then handed the letters and dictaphone tape to the secretary for her to type out my replies. After a while, I noticed she suddenly stopped typing and, looking round at me, indicated that the tape machine had switched off. I went across to her and, after checking the machine, decided that the fuse must have gone. So, without further ado, I pulled out my trusty Swiss Army knife and took the cover off the 13amp plug. Wouldn't you just credit it! As I pulled out the fuse the door opened and the electricians' shop steward walked in on his way through to the spares department. He spotted what I was doing and immediately went into Alex Scobie's office where, in a loud voice, he demanded that I be reprimanded for "taking the bread out of their mouths," a favourite union saying. Alex beckoned me into his office and I was given the opportunity to apologize directly to the shop steward for my misdemeanour. The dictaphone would now have to wait, inoperative, until an electrician could find time to come to the service office and fit a new fuse. To say that I was boiling inside was an understatement ...

There were quite a few problems which caused stoppages at Meriden in the early Seventies and each stoppage was another nail in Triumph's coffin. Quite often unions would accuse each other of poaching members, which usually caused an almighty uproar at shop-floor meetings with people shouting and threatening each other. The atmosphere slowly got worse and strikes were called by the officials without even a shop-floor meeting at which the members could vote on the prevailing issue. It wasn't uncommon to see a shop steward or works convenor simply walk along a line of chaps working at their benches, tap each on their shoulder and say "You're out on strike." I was affected before I went on to staff and, as a young chap with a wife, kids and mortgage, it was the last thing in the world I wanted! Anyway, enough of that — back to the bikes.

Where there's a will ...

The last of the oil-in-frame 650s were coming off the line with the new five-speed gearbox and we were soon in trouble with the breakage of the cruciform cog which caused all sorts of problems. A redesign quickly cured this, but all production was now committed to the Americas and what few parts were coming up to the spares department were, without exception, made ready for despatch to overseas dealers. This put an intolerable strain on myself and my new colleague, Jeff Wright, in a way I'll explain.

To appreciate how the system worked, I'll run through a typical sequence whereby a chap with a new bike suffers a breakdown on some part or other. He would take the bike to his dealer who, after dismantling and inspection, would send in the offending part together with a guarantee claim duly filled in with the relevant particulars of the bike. On the claim would be the name of the dealer, the bike's engine and frame numbers, date of purchase and the customer's name and address. We could then process the claim so that the dealer would receive a set payment for his work, and pass the spare part request to the spares department so that it could despatch a replacement. It was then up to the dealer to get the bike put back together with the new part and the customer mobile. But - and it was a big but - since all the available parts were already earmarked for despatch, usually to America because of the failures over there (you could see a bin full of the part you wanted but you couldn't have one), it sometimes took weeks to get what you needed. Jeff and I were making excuses every day to irate customers and dealers as to why the parts were not forthcoming. Sometimes the customers would by-pass their dealer and come to the service counter, demanding the part they had been waiting for. As Jeff and I became more and more frustrated, I went down to the works manager's office and asked to see him on this subject. After sitting and talking to him, I could see that I wasn't going to get anywhere on the spares scarcity problem so, in desperation, I rose from my seat and said "How the hell do you tell a chap with a six-week-old bike, who's been waiting for a part under warranty for a month, that there is no promise of a replacement in the foreseeable future?" The works manager looked at me with a supercilious grin on his face and said "That's not my job, it's yours!" With that I turned, walked out of the office and resolved to take drastic action, whether anyone liked it or not!

I'd been dealing with the problem so far by sorting out the worst six cases: in other words, the half dozen who had been waiting the longest. It was usually just the one item which failed, resulting in a run on that item but, as I've said, *every example of the part that came out of the machine shop would go straight into production to keep the track going.* In the instance that springs to mind, it was the 650 duplex clutch chain wheel that we had problems with, but what the problems were I can't remember. However, there was a bin full of them in the spares stores, but they were all booked out to American dealers and could not be touched. I decided to myself that I'd simply got to go down into production after knocking-off time and pinch six! I took a cardboard box and waited until after 4.30pm when the main factory had finished (by now working hours were shorter). The service and spares staff and the staff in the stores, including the two girls on the packing section, didn't finish until 5.15pm, which gave me some time to carry out my sortie down into the factory, pinch the parts, get them back to one of the packing girls and have them parcelled up whilst I made out address labels to the customers' respective dealers. The parcels would then go out at about 5.00pm to the GPO in the works van and, hopefully, the customers' bikes would soon be back in operation. I'd made sure that the parcels had gone before going back into the service office, only to be met by a glaring Alex Scobie, who beckoned me into his office. I'd been seen leaving the track with my plunder by someone who had 'phoned him. He wasn't amused and it's the one and only time he gave me a dressing down. I'd got to the point where I didn't much care what happened to me and told him that I wasn't prepared to lie to customers any more. I also said that, as no-one else seemed to care, if the situation arose again I'd have no hesitation in doing the same! He looked at me from behind his desk, screwed up his steely eyes and said "Okay mate, just don't get caught next time!"

I half smiled and came out of his office, knowing full well that what I was doing was morally right. I resolved to do whatever was required should similar circumstances arise again — and they did! In some cases, I'd even get the parts packed and take them home, posting them from the General Post Office in my town, just in case someone in the stores was keeping a check on outgoing mail. It was a helluva way to run a ship, but we'd absolutely got to get the bikes back on the road or their owners would never buy Triumph again.

Due to the growing number of warranty claims, we now had a full-time warranty clerk in the service office whose sole occupation was checking them through. They had to be correlated and then entered on to a computer at Armoury Road, so he was dodging between Meriden and Birmingham several times a week. It gave me an awful feeling to see him enter the office with huge piles of printouts — all guarantee claims - which meant money that had to be paid out for work that was under warranty. At one point, I reckon we were giving away about £12 with each and every bike. Alex and I were using all our wits to get over the problems by fair means or foul, but to no avail. Under these circumstances we couldn't win!

By September 1973, the Norton-Villiers-Triumph takeover had happened and industrial action resulted in the factory closing and the shop-floor workers being made redundant, with only the service, spares and experimental de-

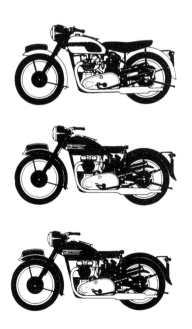

partments being retained. It wasn't unusual for me to have to answer a 'phone call from a customer who had turned up on his bike for warranty work to be carried out on the day appointment system, only to be denied access to the factory by the union pickets on the main gate. He would leave his bike in front of the gates and walk up to the telephone box at the corner of Albert Road,

Alex Scobie, Len Bayliss and Bob Manns mounted, with ET standing extreme left, at Montlhery, France, in 1949.

ringing the service office to tell us that he'd arrived but couldn't get in! I would then make my way through the deserted finishing shop and outside to the gates, where I'd have to argue the toss with the pickets in an effort to get the customer and his bike on to the premises. A lot of resentment built up over the next few weeks, with just a handful of us trying to keep the service and spares functions going. It couldn't last, it was an impossible situation.

It was usual for us to be prevented from leaving with our vehicles until we had been subjected to a search by the pickets. If I was riding my Tiger Cub it wasn't too bad, as all they did was look inside my lunch bag. If driving a car, however, the pickets would not move the barricade until you had got out of the vehicle and they had looked through the inside, under the bonnet and in the boot. If they wished, you also had to submit to a personal search "in case you were removing important papers," so they said. On the final fateful morning, I arrived at the factory gates, only to be met outside by my colleagues who all stood around in a group by their vehicles, lined up on the side of the road. The gates were now barricaded with corrugated tin sheets and it was obvious from the shouting going on behind them that we were not going to get in. At this point, I knew it was all over for the Triumph Engineering Company Limited. The dream was dead.

Alex Scobie, that dear old soul who, in 1949, had ridden the Thunderbirds at Montlhery in France for their launch, along with the other greats — Alan Jefferies, Bob Manns and Len Bayliss — who had lapped hour after hour in excess of 90mph for 24 hours, looked at me with tears in his eyes and said "Well, mate, we'll just have to play it by ear now, won't we?"

Years later, I asked Alex how he managed to lap so consistently when crouched so low over the tank; after all, I remarked, the 1949 Thunderbird would go quicker than 90 to 93mph,

Alex and the author in 1990 at Coombe Park during shooting of a Tiger 100 for a magazine article.

so therefore it must have been extremely difficult to accurately control the bike on the twistgrip at just that speed! He looked at me with a twinkle in those steely eyes and said "Simple, mate." On all three bikes - JAC769, 770 and 771 - a few turns were taken off the throttle outer cable so as to generate quite a bit of slack — about half to three-quarters of an inch. By going out on each bike in turn, first on a warm-up lap, then flat-out with the twistgrip 'on the stop', it was found that the top speed was below 90mph. So, by taking up a few threads on the cable adjuster, it was possible to accurately set the speed to stay at between 90 and 93mph on a flat-out throttle. Quite ingenious, I thought.

One of the problems the riders encountered on their journey to France was a slipping clutch on one of the three bikes. Re-adjustment couldn't cure it, so the only recourse was to dismantle the primary transmission on the roadside in some small French village. In 1949, all Triumphs were equipped with cork-insert clutch plates (steel plates with windows in them and each window had a cork insert). The three riders examined the plates and decided to make some new cork inserts from wine bottle corks! From what I can gather, they had to drink six bottles of local plonk to get enough corks to do the job. Alex reckoned all three bikes fairly flew the last few kilometres to Montlhery! From all accounts of that epic ride — Alex was most modest — it required superhuman effort to hustle three standard sprung-hub 6T Thunderbirds along at speeds in excess of 90mph for 24 hours. After the stint, the three bikes were ridden all the way back to Meriden and stopped off at the Arc de Triomphe in Paris for their picture to be taken for publicity purposes. Back at Meriden, the bikes were put up on workbenches and, in the presence of the FIM officials, the engines were stripped and measured to assess wear and damage. All three

bikes passed with flying colours!

Dear old Alex, he is the most extraordinary motorcyclist I've ever known. He road-tested all the GP models at very high road speeds along the old A45 from Meriden to Daventry, often having ding-dongs with the Norton boys who used the same stretch of road. Some of his stories were absolutely hair-raising and kept audiences, on our nights out to various motorcycle clubs, on the edge of their seats. He would, where the road permitted, take the bike up to 7200rpm in top gear, which gives a road speed of between 115 and 120mph! And this was on low octane fuel, the only stuff available just after the war in 1948.

He was as hard as iron, having undergone two open-heart operations. He seemed invincible. During his Army service in the Second World War, he re-

One of Scobie's 'babies,' the actual Ernie Lyons 1946 Manx Grand Prix machine. The author has the original test report by Alex Scobie.

ceived a congratulatory letter from Winston Churchill for his clandestine activities behind enemy lines. In my presence he faced down six hooligans at a motorway service area, which was the only time I really wanted to be somewhere else. We had been out to give a talk to a London section of the Triumph Owners Motorcycle Club. On the way home, at about 11 o'clock, we decided to stop at the motorway services on the M1. For some reason best known to Forte, one side of the service area was closed, so we had to cross to the other side via the overhead walkway. It was 1972 and coming up to Christmas, so both of us were wearing topcoats; me in my ordinary Dunn and Co. and Alex in his three-quarter length sheepskin. We always used to joke that it looked like the one worn by General Grivas, the EOKA terrorist leader in Cyprus during the troubles over there in 1956.

As we started down the steps on the other side of the motorway, we were suddenly faced with half a dozen young chaps coming up towards us. They were obviously out for trouble, as one of them said something like "There's two, let's get 'em!" Alex was two steps down from the top when he stopped dead, I instantly stopped one step up from him and to his right. By now I was gently peeing myself with fear but Alex, dear old Alex, with his steely eyes said "Okay, who's going to be the first to come and get it?" With that, he took up a fighting stance of left foot forward and right hand cocked. I thought "Oh God, what are you doing Alex?" But the young chaps faltered and, seeing this, I advanced one step below where Alex was standing and adopted an aggressive posture, saying something like "You take those three and I'll see to these." With that we advanced down the steps and, to my undying relief, the six turned and ran! I would never have done anything like it but for that

Alex Scobie and Percy Tait on the author's stand, International Classic Bike show, 1990. Note the photos from 1949 and 1954 on the board behind.

old man, who remained my firm friend, accompanying me to many a motorcycle show right up to his untimely death. He knew he didn't stand much of a chance during his third open-heart operation but he gave the go-ahead, nonetheless, and succumbed whilst still under the anaesthetic, never regaining consciousness. Dear old Alex, man of iron, good friend, God bless.

Epitaph

Walking away from the factory for the last time after all those years caused a great emotional change in me and I really didn't want to know about bikes, especially Triumphs, any more. It really was a bad time to be out of work; Edward Heath was Prime Minister, his Conservative government about to be brought down by the miners and, as well as everywhere being on a three day week, there were electricity cuts due to coal shortages at the power stations. I'd just about given up finding any work when an opportunity in the local foundry, which made cast aluminium car wheels, presented itself. It was an awful job, working stripped to the waist in temperatures over 100 degrees Fahrenheit. It was so hot, we were supplied with salt tablets and lemon and barley water, free, every hour on the hour. The job lasted about six months until the miners' strike caught up with the foundry and the Standard Triumph car plant, for whom we were making the wheels, and I was out of work again!

All the while that I'd been working at the foundry, I'd been reading pieces in the national and local papers about the workers' co-operative, the money that it wanted from the National Enterprise Board and all the various reasons why Triumph shouldn't be allowed to die. The co-operative was set up by union convenors, shop stewards and staunch members, who thought that, with financial help from the government, a Soviet-type 'all for one and one for all' operation could be successful. Its occupation of the Meriden site had been condoned by Labour left-wingers of the day and the full-time union officials from Coventry, with the statement that "We can sell as many as we can build" constantly being quoted to the media. Over a year had gone by since the occupation began, and Dennis Poore had been persuaded to leave the workers with the B range model to build. Yet this was the model which had caused most of the warranty problems in the first place and, even before Meriden closed, there were thousands of unsold T120RVs and TR6RVs stockpiled in America. The Honda four-cylinder 750cc motorcycle had knocked us badly, offering smoothness, quietness, an electric start and absolutely no oil leaks.

Tales of Triumph & Meriden

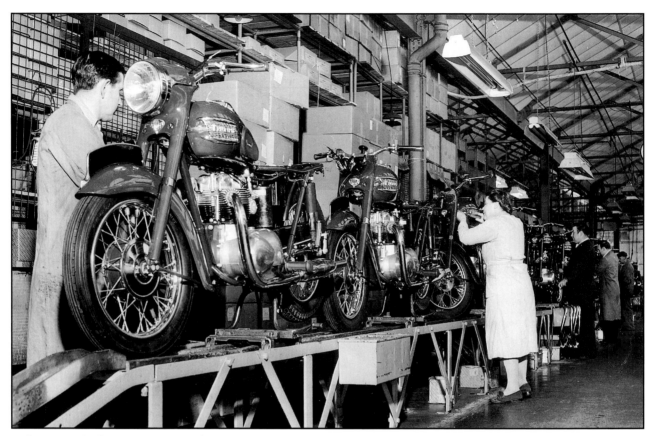

The twin cylinder, or B range, track in 1961. A 'clock' suspended above the workers showed, at a glance, the number of machines produced.

What was worse, was that it was about the same price! I thought at the time that by selling about 96 per cent of our total output to the North Americas, we were putting all our eggs in one basket, and now both handles had come off that basket! I wondered who had waved the magic wand and cured all the problems so these two models would now sell, as the public were repeatedly told they would be by the co-op spokesmen.

I was so incensed by it all, especially thinking back to the amounts of warranty money we had been giving away, specifically on the two models in question, that I resolved to write to the local paper and one of the nationals, both of which were carrying regular stories on the co-operative's progress. My letter simply stated, more or less, what I have written here, detailing the problems with the 650cc models as well as the unsold bikes in the States. I didn't get a reply from the local newspaper editor, but the editor of a national daily did reply, only to say "In the interests of political expediency we will not be publishing your letter." That's when I thought "Let it go" ...

Apart from riding my little Tiger Cub to and from my new job as an engineer at the Motor Industries Research Association, where Percy, Whistle, Stan and I did the Pave tests, I didn't think about bikes much at all, until a mysterious telephone call one Saturday morning in 1977 rekindled my interest. It was

Another view of the B range track in 1961 with 6T Police machines followed by American Bonnevilles.

TRIUMPH TIGER 650

The other B range 650cc model to run into trouble was the Tiger 650.

from a man setting up the new National Motorcycle Museum at Bickenhill who wanted me to go and work for him. After long and serious talks with my wife, Glo, I decided to leave MIRA and take him up on his offer. Suddenly, I was back amongst bikes again, restoring mainly Triumphs but with other odd types thrown in for when the new museum finally came to fruition and opened its doors to the public. I suppose I restored getting on for thirty bikes, the 1000cc Triumph Quadrant prototype being one of them. When I finally left in 1982 to start my own little one-man restoration business, I decided to employ the techniques and training I had received at Meriden all those years ago. It was my son-in-law who suggested that I ought to put it on to video cassette and, from

Tales of Triumph & Meriden

The author's Speed Twin at the NEC Motorcycle Show.

The Meriden site in 1982: Bonneville Close (top) and Daytona Drive.

this suggestion, came two three-hour workshop manual videos. As he put it "When you drop off the perch, at least we've got something to look back at!"

I also received a telephone call from the BBC tv unit which was making a documentary for BBC2 called *Design*. It dealt mainly with what the title implies, but it also looked at the demise of the British motorcycle industry through lack of foresight and design improvements. It coincided with the demolition of the Meriden site to make way for a housing estate. I had to turn up on the day, mounted on my 1953 Speed Twin and ride it through the smoke and rubble. An interview of thirty minutes' duration was cut back to something like 15 seconds, but I didn't mind really, as I had been the last person in the world to ride a Triumph on the shop-floor of Meriden before it was gone for ever! It was possibly the saddest day of my life.

In my years of restoring bikes, I've made some good friends, met a lot of old friends from Triumph and built bikes for customers the old-fashioned way. It gives me a great deal of pleasure to use my original spanners from Meriden, tighten down a cylinder head and adjust the tappets just the way we used to do it in the service repair shop. I don't suppose I'll ever stop working on old Triumphs, especially the sprung hub models. I suppose you could say that I've got a Tiger by the tail!

The author as last man to ride through the ruins of the Meriden factory on a Triumph motorcycle. This shot was taken during filming for the BBC2 programme Design, *which documented the demolition of the Meriden site.*

Index

Tales of Triumph & Meriden